THE FLAG HERITAGE FOUNDATION MONOGRAPH

PUBLICATION No. 8

THE SUN AND THE LION
AS SYMBOLS OF
THE REPUBLIC OF MACEDONIA
A HERALDIC AND VEXILLOLOGICAL ANALYSIS

by Jovan Jonovski, MTh, MA, PhD, AIH

Edward B. Kaye, Editor

FLAG
HERITAGE
FOUNDATION
DANVERS, MASSACHUSETTS
2020

THE FLAG HERITAGE FOUNDATION
MONOGRAPH AND TRANSLATION SERIES

The Flag Heritage Foundation was established in 1971 in order, among other purposes, "to collect, organize, and disseminate information concerning all aspects of flags and related symbols" and "to promote wide public knowledge of the rich history of flags which fosters international understanding and respect for national heritage." It is a registered charity in the Commonwealth of Massachusetts.

The Flag Heritage Foundation Monograph and Translation Series was established in 2009 to publish monographs on flags and related subjects, and to translate and publish in English works previously appearing in languages inaccessible to many scholars. This is the eighth publication in the Series.

Price: US $15 (plus shipping)
Non-profit organizations, libraries, and vexillological and heraldic organizations
may obtain copies *gratis* or at a reduced rate – inquire of the Foundation.

CONTENTS

Ceremonial hoisting of the flag of the Republic of Macedonia
in front of the Parliament Building, 19 September 2017.

PREFACE

My love for heraldry began during my visits to Poland in the late 1970s and 1980s, when I bought stickers and pins with coats of arms. But I forgot that childhood enthusiasm, only to rediscover heraldry during my studies in Budapest 1994 and London 1995. Coming from a country with practically no public heraldry, I encountered a world of heraldic abundance; I bought my first books on the subject and began to learn the art and science of heraldry.

My interest in flags came later, through heraldic flags and years studying heraldry. I launched my first website, "Heraldry in Macedonia," in 2000 and founded the Macedonian Heraldry Society in 2003.

After some two decades of interest and study of heraldry I wanted to enroll in doctoral program. I insisted doing it in Macedonia but could not find suitable advisor. All the professors I asked declined, saying their fields were too distant from heraldry and vexillology, so I had to postpone my doctoral studies.

Then, realizing that very little had been written on the subject, I published *Symbols of Macedonia* in 2015. In studying the theory of symbols for that book, I entered another world of symbolic meaning and human responses to it. I knew that the book should not be just historical review of the presence of the symbols through history. I had a tight schedule and much to cover, but it sufficed as the first such book in Macedonia, and in it I asked other researchers to pursue more specific in-depth studies.

Luckily, I then met Prof. Dragica Popovska, an anthropologist from the Institute of National History, who already had published several works on symbolism using modern anthropological and social approaches to the symbolic meaning of monuments. She agreed to serve as my advisor. Under her guidance my work—which started as purely heraldic and vexillological—began to include the political, social, economic, and above all the idealistic influences in the process of obtaining and developing the arms and flags of groups, nations, and states. I deeply appreciate the work and effort she put into all phases of its development, without which my thesis would have had much less importance. I am very grateful for her patience and thoroughness in repeated readings of the entire thesis with great sense for detail.

I also want to thank two people who blazed the trail before me in writing doctoral theses in the field, whose experience and conversations were indispensable: Dr. Željko Heimer, president of the Croatian Heraldic and Vexillological Association, and Dr. Tijana Trako Poljak, both from Zagreb, Croatia. I also thank Dr. Stojan Antonov, president of the Bulgarian Heraldic and Vexillological Society, for his invaluable advice and insights on many issues that arose as I wrote my thesis.

For reasons of economy much of the bibliography referencing untranslated Macedonian sources is presented in Cyrillic charactersis without Latin transcription or English translation. I would like to acknowledge Ted Kaye, my American copy-editor, for his months of generous and painstaking work putting this book in order and making it sound English (or at least American) and Stan Contrades for proofreading the text. I am also grateful to David F. Phillips, and the Flag Heritage Foundation, for making the publication of this book possible.

This monograph is an abridged version of my doctoral thesis *The Sun and Lion as Symbols in the Heraldry and Vexillology of Macedonia*, defended on 12 July 2018, at the University of SS. Cyril and Methodius, Institute of National History, Skopje, Macedonia. The defense commission was headed by Prof. Dr. Todor Čepreganov, followed by the mentor, Prof. Dr.

Dragica Popovska, and members Prof. Dr. Katerina Mirčevska, Prof. Dr. Biljana Ristovska-Josifovska, and Prof. Dr. Maja Angelovska-Panova.

The theoretical part of the thesis along with its sociological and anthropological portions is omitted and the extensive discussion of Macedonian civic heraldry is summarized only briefly; the focus here is on the sun and the lion as symbols and their use on flags and coats of arms connected to Macedonia. The research covers three periods: from before the formation of the Macedonian state to 1944, then from 1944 to independence in 1991, then from 1991 to the present. The topic is multidisciplinary, taking into account the ethnological, historical, social, sociological, legal, and political aspects of the subject.

The resulting work presented here provides the lay reader and the scholar a comprehensive review of Macedonia's use of two vitally important symbols: the sun and the lion, through the millennia to today. While based on my academic work, it is also informed by my personal involvement in proposals for arms and flags for my country. I hope this book answers many questions while supporting and inspiring future research.

Jovan Jonovski
Skopje

A NOTE FROM THE EDITOR

It has been an honor and a pleasure to work closely with the author to help guide this important monograph into print, especially during this era of great change for the Macedonian people. Making it widely accessible in English enhances its value to vexillologists (and humanities scholars in general) worldwide.

We faced many decisions and alternatives when choosing the style of this text, ultimately settling on some key principles—for example, we use American English spelling and vocabulary. We adopted the word "gold" to denote the color, even though purists might insist on "golden," we present heraldic blazons using modern language to make them more accessible to readers, we used digits rather than spelled-out numbers to identify centuries, and we chose not to convert the country's name to "North Macedonia," as the dissertation predates that momentous change in February 2019.

Translating into English from Macedonian (a language with a different sentence structure, extensive inflection, and three definite articles but no indefinite article) can pose a significant challenge, but one I hope we have overcome. The test of the copy-editor is to identify and correct any lapses in fully transmitting the intended meaning. To the extent any such lapses remain, the fault is not the author's, but mine.

Ted Kaye
Portland, Oregon

INTRODUCTION

Macedonia is situated on the Balkan Peninsula in southeast Europe. Reflections of European heraldic practices emerged in the Balkans below the Danube River in the 13th century and the first half of the 14th century, with a few rulers using arms. As noted by Ацовиħ, 2008, this was "heraldry of emblems, not of rules." However, Macedonia soon came under the control of the Ottoman Empire, beginning an era in which the Islamic proscription of the use of images eliminated any real possibility of bearing arms or flying flags.

The Macedonian national movement started in the second part of the 19th century, with several uprisings against Ottoman rule—from Razlovci in 1876 through Ilinden in 1903. The first proposal for a flag for independent Macedonia originated in 1914 in the Macedonian colony in St. Petersburg, Russia.

The Ottoman period ended with the Balkan wars (1912–13) and the partition of Macedonia between Serbia (Vardar Macedonia), Bulgaria (Pirin Macedonia), and Greece (Aegean Macedonia). The Macedonians who longed for reunification considered this an occupation. The territory of the modern-day Republic of Macedonia was absorbed by the Kingdom of Serbia; after the First World War it was incorporated into the Kingdom of Serbs, Croats, and Slovenes (later renamed Yugoslavia).

Democratic Federal Macedonia was formed during the first session of the Anti-Fascist Assembly for the National Liberation of Macedonia (ASNOM) on 2 August 1944 (it later became the People's Republic of Macedonia, a federal unit of the Federal People's Republic of Yugoslavia). It chose a Soviet-style state emblem; its flag was red with a red five-pointed star fimbriated in gold.

The choice of an emblem sends a message, through its form and its content. The design of a symbol to represent a national identity is a product of specific socio-political events that surround its adoption, as a process of wider social forces that extend beyond national borders (Cerulo 1995, 2). The choice of national symbols is a process in which a symbol or a symbolic composition is selected from a multitude of possible symbols. Through their application, promotion, creation story, repetition, continuity, and significance, they are further constructed as national symbols—crucial for building the identity of a political nation.

The choice of symbols for the coat of arms and the flag is not unambiguous, in the sense that there is no single symbol, or one symbolic composition, which represents the nation perfectly. It requires a process to select not only a symbol, but also a specific design. Symbols may be chosen or designed in a closed process where work is given to one designer, entrusted to a small team of experts (the traditional approach), or conducted through a public competition. When selecting a symbol, the primary message that needs to be communicated is considered the most important.

Scholars (Laswell, Lerner, Sola Pool 1952, 15) distinguish among three categories of national symbols or emblems:

a) Symbols of identification—e.g., with traditional or historical heritage;

b) Symbols of preference—e.g., freedom, independence, fraternity, justice, etc.; and

c) Symbols of aspirations or expectations—e.g., progress, the inevitability of a world revolution, the proletariat (an icon of an economic class), etc.

In Europe, most state coats of arms fall into the first category, with all national emblems until 1948 being selected in the traditional way. This approach requires historical research to find symbols, insignias, or emblems that were used to represent a state or ruler that can be traced as part of the national myth of the "new" state.

The coats of arms of the neighbors of the Republic of Macedonia were adopted in the 19th century and first half of the 20th century: those of the Principality of Serbia (1835),[1] and the Kingdom of Bulgaria (1879)[2] were taken from the *Stemmatographia* of Vitezović of 1701, and that of the Republic of Albania (1912)[3] was taken from historic Illyrian arms. The coat of arms of Greece underwent several changes, from an ancient composition to a simple cross.[4]

Two symbols, the sun and lion, have been used in Macedonia from the Bronze Age to the present. They appear on various objects—such as coins, ceramics, jewelry, costumes—as well as in the spiritual sphere, that is, in myths and songs. They were used on coats of arms and flags in and connected with Macedonia as symbols of territory and collective identity. The lion was mainly used as a symbol on coats of arms and flags from the Middle Ages to the early 20th century, in connection with the arms attributed to Alexander the Great of Macedonia. The sun as a symbol was used on the coats of arms and flags in Macedonia from the beginning of the 20th century, mainly as a symbol of freedom and an emerging new world system.

A country's coat of arms, flag, and anthem are not only official state symbols themselves, but also bearers of symbolism that serves to legitimize the system over a long period, so that it becomes "natural" by building agreement on the basic meaning of symbols among its members. The symbolic design of national identity is a product of specific socio-political events that surround the adoption of the symbol.

The coat of arms and the flag are symbols of group identity and authority, symbolic representations of common values and continuity of existence, which enable coordination of action, collective memory, tradition, and history. Through coats of arms and flags, individuals

---

[1] It was Stojan Novaković's idea to establish a symbolic connection in the arms of the new Kingdom of Serbia, showing continuity with the medieval Serbian state of Tsar Dušan. In 1882 the two-headed white eagle (from the coat of arms of the noble Nemanjić family in the Illyrian Armorials) was added and the arms of the Principality of Serbia placed on the eagle's breast. The design, by Austrian Ernst Krahl, was later reintroduced in 2009.

[2] In 1997, the design of the coat of arms of the Kingdom of Bulgaria of 1927–1946 was restored, with minimal changes to the crown, in an interpretation by Kiril Gogov and Georgi Chapkanov.

[3] The arms of Albania were derived from the arms of the Kastrioti family. The flag (actually a heraldic banner) was adopted on 28 November 1912 based on a proposal by Ismail Qamil. In 1992 the Republic of Albania restored the small arms of 1930; in 1998 Skanderbeg's helmet in gold was placed in the chief of the shield.

[4] In 1822 the emblem depicted the goddess Athena with an owl. In 1828 it used a phoenix, born again from the ashes, with a cross above and the date "1821" below (the phoenix was also used from 1967 to 1975). Between these periods a coat of arms—blue with a silver cross—was used, with additional dynastic elements from the coats of arms of the ruling dynasties. On 7 June 1975 a new coat of arms was introduced—blue with a silver cross—with the shield surrounded by two laurel branches, designed by Costas Gramatopoulos.

are bound together with the wider political system, and therefore such symbols are crucial for the functioning of the political system.

The choice of a symbol for a coat of arms and/or a flag is a process in which a specific symbol or symbolic composition is selected from among a wide range of possible symbols. These are then presented and built on further. The choice of the emblem depends on the social context that favors one symbol at the expense of others. In this way, symbols that were once suppressed may be elevated, which may sometimes lead to a perception of these symbols as being of greater value.

1. The Sun and the Lion in the Arms and Flags of Macedonia before 1944

The sun—the dominant source of creative energy in most cultures and often the perceived center of the universe—has always fascinated people. It is rich in meaning, and at the same time it can represent a multitude of ideas, a source of meanings with complex symbolism. As a source of heat it symbolizes passion, courage, and eternal youth. As a source of light it is a symbol of knowledge and truth. The sun represents the day, and therefore of the measurement of time and marking events on Earth. And because of its power and cyclicality, it is considered a deity in many cultures.

The sun appears as a deistic symbol in the Bible and in the Qur'an, but negatively because in the monotheistic religions it is considered blasphemy to worship the sun instead of the one God (Yahweh or Allah). In this context, the sun is mentioned in 16 verses in the Bible and in 3 verses in the Qur'an.

For ancient Macedonians, the sun was a symbol of royal power. The origin of Macedonia's royal Argead dynasty is related to the sun, as recounted by Herodotus. He wrote how three brothers—Gauanes, Aeropus, and Perdiccas (the forefather of the Argead dynasty)—worked for the king of the Illyrians. When they demanded their salary, the king showed them where the sun's rays fell on the floor, saying "this is all you deserve". Perdiccas outlined the sun's projection on the floor with a knife, then "drew the sunlight to his bosom" three times. Thus, the sun is considered a symbol of the divine origin of the royal power derived from the sun god (Проева 2004, 125). In addition, the ancient Paeonians (a kingdom later incorporated into Macedonia) had a cult of the sun, which they honored in the form of a disk placed atop a long vertical spear.

For the ancient Slavs, the sun symbolized the most revered god who appeared in several forms: Svarog, the god of the sun, and therefore of earthly fire; his son Svarožič, also the god of the sun; and Daybog, the god of the day, thus connected to the sun. Thus, the three deities of the ancient Slavs related to the symbol of the sun (Вражиновски 2015, 41).

Macedonian folk beliefs, which intertwine with Christian traditions, see the sun as a symbol of the deity, considering it his offspring. For the Macedonian people, the sun also symbolizes purity, beauty, and goodness. So in everyday speech the terms a "clear" sun or a "golden" sun are used. While the sun is perceived as a positive symbol, its "reddening" can portend misfortune.

The sun has been used as a symbol with multiple meanings in Macedonia from ancient times to the present, when it appears in the state emblem (officially called the coat of arms), the flag, and the anthem—in them the rising sun appears as a symbol of freedom, a new beginning, and a better tomorrow.

The cult of the sun may date from the end of the Bronze Age. The sun as a symbol of fertility is found on "Macedonian bronzes"—jewelry—depicted as a circular motif in the form of a stylized wheel which Paeonian priestesses wore on their belts in the 8th and 7th centuries BC.

A 16-rayed sun of the Kutleš (Vergina)[5] type appears at the bottom of 12 ceramic wine cups from Ohrid. A 12-rayed sun of this type is depicted in the center of Macedonian shields from a tomb in Bonče, near Prilep, dating from the 4th century BC, while in the seven semicircular fields around the shield the suns are 8-rayed (Кузман et al 2013, 676). However, this sun is most recognizable in the shape found on the lid of the sarcophagus from the royal tomb in Kutleš (Vergina).

The sun, known as the symbol of eternity, appears on the bottom of the cups of Vardarski Rid (an archaeological site near Gevgelija) from the 2nd and 1st centuries BC: a 6-rayed sun inside two concentric circles, surrounded by six doubled half-circles.

Figure 1 – Trihemiobol
of Derrones

The 8-rayed sun, a symbol of the sun god, is depicted on the reverse of a trihemiobol coin of Derrones (479–460/450 BC) (Fig. 1), as well as on a bronze coin of the Paeonian king Leon (278/7–250? BC), above a demi-lion. It also appears on the shield held by the goddess Athena on a tetradrachm of Philip V (Pavlovska 2012, 17, 23, 53).

The 8-rayed sun is part of a Macedonian shield—a composition of a central solar symbol with six or seven other solar symbols distributed along the edge, which are rounded, but are often not in closed circles. They are found on coins minted by Antigon II Gonata (268–262 BC) and on a tetradrachm of Philip V (221–179 BC).

The Macedonian shield with eight divergent rays and a wreath appears on a shield from the tomb of Lison and Kalikles in Meiza, dating from the first half of the 4th century BC, as well as in frescoes in the same tomb (around the 2nd century BC) (figure 20 in Hatzopoulos & Lukopoluos, 1980).

In Byzantium the sun continued as a powerful symbol. The eight- or 16-rayed sun is found in paintings, as on the shields of the six holy warriors in St. Panteleimon Church in Nerezi, near Skopje (from the 12th century) (Jonovski 2009, 24), as well as in later frescoes in St. Andrea, Matka, near Skopje, on the facade of St. George Church in Staro Nagoričane, near Kumanovo (both from the 14th century) (Апостолова, 2009, 199), and in St. George Church in Lazarovci, Kičevo, from the 16th century (Јоновски, 2015, 32).

The solar symbol decorates women's regalia from Macedonia, such as the *pafta*, a form of circular metal jewelry worn on the belt, and the *tepelak*, a bridal headdress from the Ohrid region (Пиличкова 2013, 61).

The sun, as a symbol of light and heat, appears as a rosette decorating ceilings in many traditional houses in Macedonia and represents dignity for every household. It is centered in the ceiling just as the noon sun is in the center of the sky. Such rosettes are carved from wood,

---

[5] Kutleš is the name of a Slavic Macedonian village near the ancient Aigai, the capital of the ancient Macedonian Argead dynasty. This region become part of Greece in 1912; the name was changed to Vergina in 1922.

forming a sun mostly from floral elements and usually with an odd number of rays (Намичев, 78).

* * *

The lion (*Panthera leo*) once inhabited North Africa, Southern Europe, and the Near East to India but by the end of the 1st century AD it was extinct in the South Balkans and Macedonia. The male is recognized by its mane, and since antiquity the lion has been the most widely used animal symbol in human culture.

The lion appears in the Bible as "the lion of Judah" (Genesis 49:9), a symbol of the Israelite tribe of Judah, and also as a motif decorating the approach to the throne in Solomon's palace (2 Chronicles 9:19).

Lions were common in ancient Macedonia (Packer, Clottes 2000; Nowell, Jackson 1996) and the lion is present in ancient mythology. Fighting a lion, or hunting lions, was a ritual of initiation for young Macedonian nobles (Проева 2004, 57).

In antiquity, the lion symbolized royal power. Heracles, the mythical ancestor of the Macedonians, is often portrayed fighting a lion barehanded. The royal symbolism of the lion would be used repeatedly in later history.

The image of the lion appears on an artifact from Delchevo dating from the 2nd or 3rd century—a metal wagon ornament that depicts a lion hunting a calf (Кузман et al 2013, 903). It also appears on the mosaics in Plaošnik, Ohrid.

Figure 2 – Tetradrachm of Lycceios

The lion is also found on coins. On the obverse of the Lycceios tetrobol (359–340 BC) a lion is shown in natural position for attack. A tetradrachm of the same ruler shows Heracles fighting a lion (Fig. 2). On a bronze coin of the Paeonian king Leon (278/7–250[?] BC) the lion is depicted as a demi-lion with a sun above it. The light tetrobol of Perdiccas II (454–413 BC) also depicts a demi-lion. A similar representation also appears on an obol of Archaelaos (413–399 BC). A bronze of Philip I from 244 BC shows a lion in a natural pose. A well-known image of Alexander of Macedon wearing a lion's head appears on the tetradrachm he had minted (Pavlovska 2012, 18–23).

The lion is often present on rings used by both men and women in Macedonia. The ring of Morodviz (from the second half of the 13th century or the beginning of the 14th century) shows an animal, very likely a lion, with a bent tail, surrounded by eight stars. A luxurious gilded silver cup from Orizari near Kočani, from the same period, depicts a gold lion passant on a blue background in the central part of its interior.

The lion also appears in church decorations in Macedonia—in early centuries carved on the stone parapets of the *iconostasis* (screen) and later in wood on the iconostasis itself. The lion also appears kneeling before the feet of the bishop's throne, as in the St. Jovan Bigorski Monastery (Ќорнаков, 2005, 40).

The lion as a symbol appears on ritual or wedding flags as well. It is one of the four animal symbols on the Mijaks' flag, as described by Trajčev (Filipova, 2005, 2007). The flag of the village of Ranci, Kajlari, shows two crowned lions *affronté* (facing each other). The flag is red and the lions are embroidered with white beads. Above the heads of the lions are large crowns embroidered with yellow beads. The composition has a floral border with smaller lions

11

in the corners. Above the paws of the two main lions stand the letters "B" and "A" (perhaps the initials of the bride and groom) and under the lions appears "1903."

1.1. Arms and Flags Attributed to Alexander the Great of Macedon in Medieval Europe

The image of Alexander the Great of Macedon was deeply embedded in the consciousness of the people of medieval Europe—not only as a great conqueror but also as a symbol of virtue and chivalry. Various works on his life and accomplishments appeared, notably translations and adaptations of the 3rd century *History of Alexander the Great* by Quintus Curtius Rufus and *The Life of Alexander, the King of Macedonians* by Pseudo-Callisthenes.

As heraldry flourished in the 13th century, arms were attributed to Alexander, appearing as illustrations in three types of literature: general stories, *Alexandride*s (literary works celebrating Alexander's life and achievements), and armorials. These coats of arms and armorial flags were not permanent, but various interpretations appeared depending on the region. Beginning in the 13th century, 36 original works in French and English are known, with many more medieval translations of classical works. In all of them the lion appears as a symbol in Alexander's attributed coat of arms.[6]

The first arms attributed to Alexander appeared in the early 13th century (perhaps 1210) in the work of Roger IV of Lille, *Histoire ancienne jusqu'à César*, and in its illustrated version, the manuscript of Dijon,[7] about 60 years later. In it, Alexander's coat of arms is *a silver lion on red field*; in the same era the general history of Liber Floridus[8] showed *a red lion on a silver field*.

Figure 3 – *Roman d'Alexandre*

The illustrated manuscript of *Le roman de toute chevalerie*, the 14th-century novel by Thomas de Kent about Alexander,[9] shows *a gold lion on a red field* several times (Селовски, 2016).

Of particular importance is the image of Philip II (Alexander's father) on his deathbed, dressed in a coat of arms with *a red lion on a gold field*. Perhaps it is a case of cadency, since in that period one of the main ways to create arms for younger sons was to invert the colors (Gayre 1963). From this time onward, coats of arms with *a red lion on a gold field*, and the reverse variant with *a gold lion on a red field*, would be attributed to Alexander the Great. These crossed over into the coats of arms of Macedonia, as discussed later.

In his epic poem *Les Voeux du Paon*,[10] performed before the Bishop of Liege in 1312, Jacques de Longuyon glorified "the Nine Worthies." They were a triad of triads: the "Good Pagans": Hector of Troy, Alexander the Great, and Julius Caesar; the "Good Jews":

---

[6] Attributed arms are coats of arms assigned to mythological figures, or to persons living before the beginning of heraldry in the 12th century, who did not actually bear them. They are fanciful products of the developed heraldic period.

[7] BM-ms. 0562, Dijon.

[8] BnF, ark:/12148/btv1b6000541b in the National Library in Paris.

[9] MS. Bodley 264, Bodleian Library, Oxford University.

[10] Morgan Library. MS G.24 fol. 69v.

Joshua, King David, and Judas Maccabeus, and the "Good Christians": King Arthur, Charlemagne, and Godfrey of Bouillon, King of Jerusalem. Armorials routinely included the arms of the Nine Worthies, starting in 1379 when they appeared in the armorial von den Ersten, called the *Codex Seffken*. In an 1893 edition by Gustav Adelbert Seyler, Alexander's coat of arms appears on the last page with the blazon *a gold lion on a red field within a gold engrailed bordure*.[11]

The 1338 work illustrated in Flanders by Jehan de Grise, *Roman d'Alexandre*,[12] abounds with Alexander's coats of arms—*a red lion on a gold field* in 29 illustrations, and *a gold lion on a red field* in three more (Селовски, 2016) (Fig. 3). That *gold lion on red field* also appears in the 14th century work *Mare historiarum ab orbe condito ad annum Christi 1250* by Joanne de Columna.

In addition to literary works, images of the Nine Worthies with coats of arms or armorial flags can be found in stone, frescoes, tapestries, etc. As is often the case with attributed coats of arms, these show some inconsistency (often being transposed with each other).

A gold lion holding long battle axe on a red field represents Alexander on a wool tapestry from southern Holland from about 1380. It shows the three "Good Pagans": Hector, Julius Caesar, and Alexander.[13]

The *gold lion holding an axe* appears in *Le Chevalier Errant* by Thomas III of Saluzzo, 1394, in which Alexander is represented among the Nine Worthies as a knight with a coat of arms showing *a gold lion on a red field, holding a gold axe with both paws*. In other arms, the axe turns into a halberd and sometimes the colors are reversed.

After the Bible, perhaps the book most translated and most read in medieval Europe was *Les Faicts et les conquestes d'Alexandre le Grand* by Jehan Wauquelin (†1457) (Stoneman 2008, 4). The transcriptions were richly illustrated, with variations in the artistic interpretation of the symbols, including the coats of arms. Thus Alexander's coat of arms appears as *a red lion on a gold field* in the illustrations of Willem Vereland (†1481). The same blazon is repeated in the *Blason des Armoiries* by Jerome de Bara (1540–1600), published in Geneva in 1572, and in that of Jean Robin in 1639. Coats of arms with reversed colors appear in three more instances: the Spanish arms of Garcia Alonso de Torres from 1496, the general armorial of Lauren of the 15th century, and the 1543 coat of arms of Noel Bocode (Селовски, 2016).

The earliest representation of a lion on a flag for Alexander in wall frescoes is found at Monti Castle in Italy, dating from 1430. In a depiction of the Nine Worthies holding heraldic flags; Alexander's is *a gold lion seated on a gold throne holding a gold axe on a red field*. Similar frescoes from the same period are found in the Château de Valère, in Sion, Switzerland, but there Alexander is represented by *a red lion on a gold field* (Norris *et al.* 1997, 199).

* * *

---

[11] Adolf Matthias Hildebrandt & Gustav Seyler, *Wappenbuch von den Ersten: gen. "Codex Seffken,"* Berlin (Verein Herold) 1893, available in facsimile at http://www.rambow.de/codex-seffken.html. Accessed on 1.9.2016.

[12] Ms. Bodley 264, Bodleian Library, Oxford University.

[13] Metropolitan Museum, New York. https://www.shafe.co.uk/nine_worthies_tapestry-_1380s-_new_york-_met/. Accessed on 1.9.2016.

The heraldic representations of Alexander the Great and of the King of Macedonia in European armorials are idealistic representations to glorify the "glorious" past. They appear in various books, arms, and artifacts (Jonovski 2009a).

The majority of these depict lions in one of the three heraldic poses: a lion rampant (including holding an axe) is most frequent; then a lion seated on a throne holding an axe; or, most rarely, two lions combatant. The color of the shield is usually red or gold, sometimes blue or silver. The lion, however, usually appears in gold, then red, and least often silver, blue, or black. The most common depiction is a lion rampant (with or without an axe), and in a combination of red and gold, with slightly more occurrences of *a gold lion on a red field*.[14]

The lion from the coat of arms of Alexander the Great of Macedon would later cross into the "land" coats of arms of Macedonia in armorials and Stemmatographias. The *gold lion on a red field* most commonly appears in handwritten armorials, while *a red lion on a gold field* appears most often in printed editions.

1.2. "Land Arms" of Macedonia

A "land coat of arms" refers to arms of a land as an idea, not a specific administrative territorial unit with defined borders and rulers. The emergence of land coats of arms for Macedonia and other Balkan lands resulted not only from a specific historical process but also a legal-heraldic process in the context of the Ragusa (Dubrovnik) Republic[15] and its intricate relations with the Holy League and the Ottoman Empire.[16] The movement of some families between heraldic jurisdictions (which regulated the possession of arms and their status in society) led to the creation of genealogies and armorials documenting existing and newly created arms.

Dubrovnik, like Venice, did not have a heraldic authority that granted or confirmed coats of arms—as anyone could bear a family coat of arms, such arms did not prove noble status in society. In the 15th century, many prominent citizens, merchants, citizens, and priests in the rural areas surrounding the Dubrovnik Republic began to adopt coats of arms based on examples seen in Dubrovnik (Ćosić, 2015, 20).

---

[14] Nacevski considered 35 works with heraldic illustrations for Alexander the Great; 21 are coats of arms. Nacevski, Ivan, 2016, "The Blazon of the Lion in the Attributed Arms of Alexander III of Macedon," *Macedonian Herald*, No. 10, 12-19.

[15] The Republic comprised the city of Dubrovnik and the surrounding coast including the Peljesac Peninsula and several islands, covering a territory of some 1,092 km² with a population of about 40,000, much of it engaged in maritime and related activities. (Dubrovačka Republika, http://leksikon.muzej-marindrzic.eu/dubrovacka-republika/. Accessed on 18.1. 2017.)

[16] As the main port of the western Adriatic, Dubrovnik paid tribute to the Ottoman Empire, which granted it special rights to transport goods from the Ottoman ports, increasing its power and wealth. With the formation of the Holy League in 1538, pressure from the Pope grew to join that side. With skillful diplomatic negotiations, Dubrovnik secretly promised 30 ships to the Holy League while postponing sending 50 ships to Ottoman Navy as its "vassal." The ships for the Holy League were supposedly "kidnapped," a ruse to avoid disturbing relations with the Ottomans. (Bruna Gamulin, "Dubrovačka Republika: Međunarodnopravni subjektivitet i diplomatski i konzularni odnosi," *Pravnik: časopis za pravna i društvena pitanja*, Zagreb, 49, 1 (99), 2016, 59.)

Several maritime and merchant families from Slano, near Dubrovnik, entered into the service of the Spanish emperor Carlos V (1500–1558). The first was Ivelja Grgurić, who also recruited his four sons, his sons-in-law, as well as other families with whom he was related or friendly—primarily the Dolist-Tasović, Korenić-Neorić, and Komnen families. They quickly advanced in the Spanish Armada, and thus in Spanish society, where coats of arms were a mark of nobility granted only by the crown. To have their nobility recognized, members of these families had to prove that all eight great-grandparents were of noble origin, which in practice meant that all had to have coats of arms (Соловјев 2000, 128). As a result, these families began collecting and creating genealogies, armorials, and myths about their descent. Ivelja's son, Petar, went the furthest in this process—changing his surname to Ohmučević, to relate mythically to Hrelja, a vassal of Tsar Dušan (1306–1355) with possessions in Macedonia and known in literary works and folk traditions (Палавестра 2010, 55).

These families, in order to establish connections to families from the time of the mythical "Illyrian Empire" of Tsar Dušan, needed genealogies that would bridge the gap of some ten generations over two and a half centuries. They also needed armorials to document the arms of all these families, their ancestors in both the male and female lines (Соловјев 1933, 82–87).

The resulting armorial, *Genealogies ... of the Illyrian Kingdom*, claimed to be a copy of an earlier armorial from 1340, created during the reign of Illyrian King Stefan (Dušan) Nemanjić. The author of the alleged 14th-century work was the fictional priest Stanislav Rupčić, the herald of Dušan. In this armorial there are no genealogies at all.

At that time the only way to duplicate a unique armorial was through a handwritten and hand-illustrated transcription. Through the many subsequent copies, additional arms were added, in order to give them legitimacy or simply to supplement a family genealogy. There are 23 such transcripts known, later called the "Illyrian Armorials," of which seven have been lost (Ацовић 2008, 219–220). The Illyrian Armorials,[17] in fact, constitute successive editions of an armorial of Slano families, created in the last decades of the 16th century.

The compiler of the armorial of the families of Slano, as well as his European colleagues, collected information about the coats of arms that should enter the armorial. For those families for whom he lacked historical facts, he probably made up the arms (which heraldry calls "fantastic arms")—a common practice. To make the armorial look older and more reliable, and to emphasize the power of the families represented, he supplemented the approximately 130 coats of arms of the families of Slano with the arms of several powerful rulers of the past, such as Nemanjić, Kotromanjić, Mrnjavčević, Balšić, and Kastrioti (Illyrian Armorial, 2005).

The coat of arms of Macedonia, depicted as *a gold lion on a red field*, is located in the first field of the dominion coat of arms of Stefan Dušan Nemanjić, which consisted of nine fields with land arms. Following this, the coats of arms of these lands were also shown individually.

---

[17] The name "Slano Armorials" is more accurate since its assemblers primarily wanted to prove the nobility of certain families from the surrounding area of Slano and did not have what would later be called "Illyrian ideas." Those, as a forerunner of Yugoslavism, would emerge at the beginning of the 19th century, then be strongly advanced shortly before and during the period of the Kingdom of the Serbs, Croats, and Slovenes (later named Yugoslavia). The "Land" coats of arms were shown only to illustrate the territory of the Dušan Empire, to strengthen the "reliability" of the armorial.

Macedonia's coat of arms has the same blazon as one of the most common of the coats of arms attributed to Alexander the Great (Ćosić 2015, 129; Селовски 2016).

When the Slano Armorials were created, many others were circulating in Europe. They inevitably included the coat of arms of Alexander of Macedon, as one of the Nine Worthies. Thus, the coat of arms of Macedonia was most likely inspired by the coat of arms of Alexander, which appears as *a gold lion on red field*, or *a red lion on a gold field* (Јоновски 2015, 171; Ćosić 2015, 129; Селовски, 2016). This blazon, with some changes in the secondary attributes of the lion, remained the same in most of the later copies.

One of the oldest known versions of the Slano Armorials is the London Armorial, dating from around 1590. The armorial's structure followed that of many European armorials, and shows the particular influence of Virgil Solis' armorial from 1555, which consisted of the coats of arms of the popes, the cardinals, and the dominion coat of arms of the Holy Roman Empire and the Holy See, as well as the coats of arms of the kingdoms and principalities, and the coats of arms of archbishops and bishops and noble families. The London Armorial followed the structure of Solis, but with the coat of arms of the cardinals replaced by images of saints, and the dominion coat of arms of the Holy Roman Empire replaced by the coat of arms of the mythical Illyrian empire. The arms on the dominion coat of arms appear in place of the kingdoms under the authority of the Holy Roman Emperor. Furthermore, the arms of 141 families replace the arms of the knights and other noblemen (Filipović 2009).

In the London Armorial the image for Macedonia shows, on a German-type shield, the arms *on a red field, a gold lion ensigned with a crown* (Fig. 4). The lion has a single tail. Above the shield a five-pointed "ancient" crown is decorated with precious stones.

Figure 4 – Land arms of Macedonia from the London Armorial

Today, the assertion that the Slano Armorials are transcriptions of an armorial from the time of Tsar Dušan has been rejected completely. But until the publication of Stjepan Ćosić's *Ideology of Genealogies* (Ćosić 2015), the prevailing hypothesis had held that all "Illyrian Armorials" were copied from a "protoarmorial" created by Don Pedro Ohmučević, admiral of the Spanish fleet, who died in Lisbon in 1599. Genealogical investigations indicate that in most cases the arms in this armorial represent families of Slano and the surrounding area. Ćosić's studies cast special light on the role of the Korenić-Neorić family—and other families included in its pages—in the creation of the Slano Armorials. The "Illyrian Armorials" are actually handwritten copies of a single work and can be considered supplemental editions of a book, which is important when compared with other sources. The transcripts were individual copies, often landing far from the public eye in private collections, archives, and monasteries. Their impact was far smaller than heraldic works that have been printed or even reissued many times.

Very similar to the London Armorial is the armorial of Korenić-Neorić, held by the University Library in Zagreb, and believed to date from 1595. The Macedonian coat of arms is shown three times: as a field of the dominion coats of arms of King Stefan Nemanjić, those of King Uroš, and on a separate page. Only the lion in this armorial is *armed* gold (the tongue and claws shown in gold). This armorial, unlike the London Armorial, also includes the arms of Spanish families into which the Korenić-Neorić daughters and other female descendants would marry after there were no male descendants (Ćosić 2015, 351–361).

Many Croatian, Serbian, Bosnian, Albanian, and other families used versions of this armorial as proof of their noble descent when claiming nobility before the Austrian, Venetian, and Dubrovnik authorities (Glasnik 1938, 4). Therefore, it was often copied, in part or in its entirety.

In the Althan Armorial of 1614, held by the University Library in Bologna, the Macedonian land arms are shown: *a gold crowned lion with a split tail on a red field*. A ducal crown is on the head of the lion, which is heraldically correct. The main difference is that for the first time, the lion has a *queue forchée* (split tail). The shield is of the "heater" type, with rounded lower sides meeting at a pointed shieldfoot, a style called "Gothic" in Macedonian practice. Above it reads: "Македонске земле чимери" (*Makedonske zemle chimeri*, the arms of the Macedonian land) (Матковски, 1970, 87).

The workmanship in the 1620 Belgrade Armorial 2 is very similar to the Althan Armorial. The Macedonian coat of arms in it is on a Renaissance shield. The style is very similar in the Vienna Armorial of Marko Skorojević of 1636–1638.

The Fojnica Armorial is kept in the Holy Spirit Franciscan monastery in the town of Fojnica in Bosnia and Herzegovina. (Miletić 2005) Dating is difficult, but it was made sometime in the 17th century.[18] Unlike in the other armorials, in the Fojnica Armorial the Macedonian coat of arms is simplified with a blazon: *a gold crowned lion on a red field*, the shield crowned with a so-called "Eastern" (radiant) crown (Fig. 5).

In the 1689 Olovo Armorial, from Bologna, the land arms are on a German shield with a five-pointed crown. The drawing has no color or heraldic hatching (Матковски 1970, 106).

In the Berlin Armorial, dating from the end of the 17th century, the land arms are shown as *a gold crowned lion on a red field* on a German shield. The lion's tail has been pulled up and a torch is found on it, unique to this armorial. Above the shield is a gold crown.

Figure 5 – Fojnica Armorial

In the 1740 *Kevešić Codex* the Macedonian coat of arms is on a French shield. Above the shield is a ducal crown, below it is "Macedoniae." Other later copies exist.[19]

* * *

The first printed book in which the Macedonian coat of arms appears, although indirectly, is the Benedictine Mavro Orbini's *The Kingdom of the Slavs*, published in Pesaro in 1601. It attempted to write the history of the Slavs, in the spirit of the beginning of the Pan-Slavic idea, with a mythological-epic approach to history. Orbini showed the coat of arms of each land or family before writing about it. The illustrations are line drawings, without heraldic hatching, taken from the Slano Armorials. While there is no article about Macedonia specifically, the Macedonian coat of arms appears as the fourth quarter of the arms of Stefan Nemanjić. If

---

[18] Aleksandar Solovjev concluded that it was made in 1675. Соловјев 2000, 166.

[19] For more see: Матковски, 1970, 77–147.

following the other colored versions of these arms, this should be *a red lion on a gold field*. This is a concept similar to the European heraldic heritage for the arms attributed to Alexander the Great.

A century later, the *Stemmatographia* of Vitezović appeared[20]—a collection of 54 arms of the lands perceived as Slavic at the earliest stage of Pan-Slavism and the Illyrian idea—to unite all the Southern Slavs in a kingdom called Illyria.[21] (It included no family coats of arms.) "Stemmatographia" means a collection of coats of arms—a work dedicated to land arms themselves rather than a work where the coats of arms appear only as illustrations. The 1694 manuscript is in Latin with hand-painted images (Матковски 1970, 114). It depicts Macedonia with a *red lion on gold field*, likely following Orbini. The printed edition of the *Stemmatographia* of 1701[22] is the first printed work to depict Macedonia's coat of arms explicitly.

Vitezović probably based his work on the *Münster Cosmography* and Orbini's *The Kingdom of the Slavs* (Матковски 1970, 116), showing the coats of arms in all territories in alphabetical order. Four explanatory verses in Latin appear beneath each shield. The Macedonian coat of arms has a Spanish shield with *a red lion on gold field*. The lion is uncrowned and has a single tail. The shield is crowned with a ducal crown with a superstructure of arches, decorated with precious stones. Above the arms is written "Macedonia" and below are the Latin verses:

> My golden shield is protected by red lion / Signs of royal honor of the past
> The Turk has deprived the lion of its great crown / Once it fell, it lost its honor.[23]

This alludes to the red lion used as a symbol by a great king in the past, likely Alexander the Great, which points to the continuity of this symbol and its heraldic use.

Matkovski, attempting to explain why Vitezović used *a red lion on a gold field* for Macedonia's coat of arms, rather than the reversed colors as in the handwritten Slano Armorials, gave the following hypothesis. Vitezović, when compiling his *Stemmatographia*, was cutting the coats of arms from another armorial without the inscriptions. When pasting them in, he mistakenly exchanged the images of the Macedonian and Bulgarian coats of arms. Thus above the inscription "Macedonia" he put a *red lion on a gold field* and above "Bulgaria" a *gold lion on a red field*. Matkovski argued that this "unintentional change of Vitezović" was the source of all

---

[20] Pavao Ritter Vitezović (1652–1713), born in Senj, was a writer, historian, printer, politician, and supporter of the "Illyrian idea."

[21] Illyria was a region in the western part of the Balkan Peninsula covering most of the former Yugoslavia and parts of Albania. Illyrian kingdoms existed from around 400 BC until 167 BC. They were composed of small areas in the region of Illyria. Only the Romans ruled the entire region, as the province of Illyricum and the praetorian prefecture of Illyricum. The province of Illyricum stretched from the Drillon River in Albania to Istria in the west and the Sava River in the north, with Solin (near Split) as the capital city. "Illyria" was again used for the Illyrian provinces included in Napoleon's French Empire 1809–1813, and for the Kingdom of Illyria (1816–1849), part of the Austrian Empire.

[22] Pavao Vitezović, *Stemmatographia Sive Armorum Illyricorum Delineatio, Descriptio Et Restitutio* […] (n.p., 1701).

[23] "Aurea scuta mihi rubeo protecta leone / Ad regale olim signa fuere decus/ Privavit magnum diademate Turca leonem/ Quo semel amisso totus abivit honor."

other places wherever a red lion appears and should be considered an error (Матковски 170, 112).

However, the second part of the *Stemmatographia* presents more information about each coat of arms. For the Macedonian coat of arms, it reads:

> MACEDONIA is distinguished by *red lion on gold*; which many people think was Greece's coat of arms. Before the time of Alexander the Great, the Epirotes had a red dog, and then they put the club of Heracles upright between bulls' horns. The Nemanjić kings, who carefully marked their superiority over subjugated nobles and regions, used a red lion to mark Macedonia.[24]

In addition, for the coat of arms of Bulgaria, it reads:

> BULGARIA is marked with a *gold crowned lion on red field*. In a manuscript I found a *red lion on gold*, which is thought to be of Macedonia. Apostolic kings, however, made it *a black lion on silver between a red mullet and crescent* (others tie it to Wallachia).[25]

This undermines Matkovski's theory that Vitezović accidentally switched the coats of arms of Macedonia and Bulgaria. The text makes clear that Vitezović believed the *red lion on gold* was the coat of arms of Macedonia. In creating the *Stemmatographia*, there was no exchange or correction of some "historical error" from any other arms; Vitezović simply used sources in which Macedonia's arms were a *red lion on gold*, which were abundant.

The greatest heraldic influence on the Southern Slavs was the Slavic translation of Vitezović's *Stemmatographia* by Hristofor Žefarović, published in 1741 in Vienna.[26] (The texts were partially modified in translation.) It presents the 58 land arms in alphabetical order with an explanation for each one and depicting them with heraldic hatching to denote their colors. The *Stemmatographia* was so popular that it was later even banned because of its use in nationalist activism (Анѓелкоска 2005).

When the question of a state coats of arms arose in the 19th century, all the Southern Slavs, without exception, turned to the Žefarović *Stemmatographia* for their arms. The coats of arms shown in it for Serbia and Trivijala were adopted by the Governing Council of Karađorđević's Serbia in the early 1800s (Новаковић 1884, 133). Then in 1835 after the Sretenje Constitution, the government of Miloš Obrenović took the coat of arms (a cross with four firesteels) and declared it the state coat of arms of the Principality of Serbia. Bulgaria's Trnovo Constitution of 1879 proclaimed the arms Žefarović showed for Bulgaria as the state coat of arms (Произход 1946, 10).

---

[24] "MACEDONIA rubeo leone aureum campum insignivit; quem nonnulli Graeciae stemma fuisse opinantur. Quidam rubeum Epiri molossum ante Alexandri M. tempora, post clavam Herculis inter buphali Taurive cornua erectam addiddit. Nemanidae reges rubeo usi sunt, pro Macedoniae insignibus, qui eorum proprietam in procerum suorum et provinciarum scutis diligenter observabant." *Stemmatographia.*

[25] "BULGARIA fulvo coronato leone in campo rubeo armatur. In quodam manuscripto reperi, Leonem rubrum super aureo campo: qui Macedoniae censetur. Apostolici reges nigrum faciunt, intra Stellam et Lunam rubeas (quam alii Valachiae appingunt) in campo albo." *Stemmatographia.*

[26] Hristofor Žefarović (†1753), considered the first Macedonian heraldist, was a painter, icon-painter, and engraver from Dojran.

For the Macedonian coat of arms the Žefarović *Stemmatographia* shows *a red lion on a gold field* on a Spanish shield. The lion has one tail and is not crowned. Above the shield is a royal five-pointed crown. Above the arms is "Македонїа." The verses for the arms differ: "The gold shield is covered by a red lion / As a sign of the church honor." Žefarović dedicated the arms to the church rather than the king. In the second part, however, he omitted the reference to the red lion as a mark of subjugation by the Nemanjić kings. As for the colors of the Bulgarian arms, he wrote that, in fact, "a light lion in a black field rises" and that "those who, instead of the black, put light one, make mistakes."

Furthermore, coats of arms are found on maps and in illustrated stories. In them the arms with a *red lion* from the *Stemmatographia* began to be used to represent Macedonia. For example, the *red lion* is found on the 1737 map by Johan Jakob and German Lidl, which shows in the lower left the coats of arms of the European countries, some from the Žefarović *Stemmatographia*. The *red lion on a gold field* appears in a book by Jovan Rajić (1726–1801), a monk, historian, and writer. The third volume of his work *History of the Various Slavic Peoples, and Especially the Bulgarians, Croats, and Serbs*, depicts the Macedonian coat of arms in a composition in which the coats of arms of all regions and provinces once inhabited by the Southern Slavs appear in a circle surrounding Tsar Dušan. The arms of Serbia, Bulgaria, Illyria, and the Nemanjići are on the four corners. In a ribbon above each coat of arms is the name of the land to which the land arms belongs; the colors are denoted by heraldic hatching (Матковски 170, 136).

The lion also appears as a symbol in monasteries and on flags. In the church of the Rila Monastery (the largest in Bulgaria),[27] four coats of arms appear on the northern part of the iconostasis: Serbian, Bulgarian, Bosnian, and Macedonian. The Macedonian coat of arms is on the lower row, right on the portal. It is a *red lion on gold*.

The same blazon for the Macedonian coat of arms is also used around 1851 on the Heraldic Table of Milan Simić with the local coats of arms of the Southern Slavs, placed on a tympanum with 11 columns showing 61 coats of arms and those of Tsars Dušan and Uroš—Macedonia's arms are a *red lion on gold field* on both. The description reads: "On the arms a lion rampant to the left in a gold field" (Матковски, 1970, 146).

Throughout history Macedonia's coat of arms differed from Bulgaria's, which, although also a lion, has most often been depicted in a different combination of colors. This is confirmed in the handwritten Illyrian arms, where Bulgaria is *red crowned lion on gold field*. But this has had no influence on the Bulgarian national identity; according to Bulgarian heraldists the *red lion on gold field* was never perceived as the national coat of arms in Bulgaria (Лажна 2014)

Although Matkovski asserted that only the *gold lion on red* is the real coat of arms of Macedonia, considering the sources referenced in his *Coats of Arms of Macedonia* leads to a different conclusion. Of the 31 sources, 26 are land coats of arms, 12 of them are from armorials, three from Stemmatographias, five from books, two from plates, two from flags, and two from frescoes. The lion most often appears rampant, except in the first field of the dominion arms, where it is passant. Ten lions are crowned; only three have a queue forchée. The red lions

---

[27] The Monastery of St. Ivan of Rila was built by Hrelja Ohmučević (the mythical ancestor of Don Pedro Ohmučević), who built the tower in 1335 and the church in 1343. The church that stands today was built in 1834–1837, and painted in 1844–1846 by the Razlovci and Samokov painting school.

are usually uncrowned, and only one has a queue forchée. The type of source seems to account for the difference: crowned lions or those with a queue forchée are in the armorials, other sources show the lion as crownless and with a plain tail.

Examining the colors of the lion and the shield, of the 25 arms for which colors are known, 13 have a *red lion* and 12 have a *gold lion*,[28] making the two colors nearly equally represented. After the publication of Žefarović's *Stemmatographia*, eight of the 10 sources have a *red lion*, which marks the *Stemmatographia's* huge influence on heraldic knowledge. The strict understanding—that *the gold lion on red* is the real Macedonian land coat of arms, and *the red lion on gold* is just a random mistake—has no factual nor scientific basis (Nacevski 2015). Coats of arms with red and gold lions were present in European heraldry and culture, connected in imagination from ancient times with the glorious kingdom and its great king Alexander of Macedon, two centuries before the appearance of the Slano Armorials of Grgurić-Ohmučević and Korenić-Neorić.

1.3. The Flags of the National Movement in the 19th Century

The ideals of the French Revolution of 1789—"liberty, equality and fraternity," represented by the new French blue-white-red tricolor—spread across much of continental Europe and fostered the national movements of the peoples of the Balkans.

National movements are socio-political and cultural phenomena that advocate the awakening of national consciousness, the protection of national rights, and the creation of a national state. These processes take place at several levels, including the formation of associations that promote the ideas of the national movement in various spheres, as well as uprisings as a form of armed struggle against the power of the ruling state.

These processes also require symbolic representation, which is often accomplished by the use of flags. Those of national movements can be civilian and military. Civilian flags comprise those used in peaceful conditions by associations, groups, and movements, including flag proposals adopted for newly freed countries. Military flags usually comprise the flags of units and commands of a country's armed forces, which involves standardization. However, revolutionary flags are a special category, representing irregular formations; usually their form, dimensions, and symbols are not standardized, as they occur spontaneously (cf. Tuđman 1994).

Macedonian revolutionary flags have their roots in *bayracs* (flags) of the *hajduks* (peasant irregular infantry) in which the *bayractar* (flag bearer) was a position of honor (Самарџић 1983). These revolutionary flags also have the characteristics of military flags, such as consecration, parading, and paying allegiance to the flag (Heimer 2016, 87).

The flag is sacred and held in the highest level of honor, even above the lives of members of the squad. The soldiers' obligation to the flag is "either to decorate it with new laurels of glory ... or to die as heroes defending it" (Дисциплинарен 1915). The constitution of a rebellion of the revolutionary era provides that, for the flag: "Everyone is obliged to make a bed of his body, and only then to fall. The guilty are punished with death. For the loss of the flag the

---

[28] Apart from the coat of arms from the Palinić Bosnian Armorial, where the color is not indicated, and in the 1640s the Belgrade Armorial, where the lion is silver. The Olovo Armorial is not colored, and is counted among the gold lions, following Matkovski.

21

punishment is death—including the *voyvoda* [the leader of the squad] who allowed the flag to be lost." (Иванов 1998, 38).

Macedonian revolutionary flags can be categorized into four groups according to their content:

1. Flags with religious symbols and slogans,

2. Flags with a lion as a heraldic figure,

3. Flags with a lion as a secondary figure, and

4. Other flags.

Flags from groups 2 and 3 follow, as well as one flag from group 4, where the sun appears.

Figure 6 – Razlovci flag

The first lion on a revolutionary flag reportedly appeared on the flag of the Macedonian regiment in Ukraine formed on 10 May 1759 by the Russian empress, Elisabeth Petrovna. The regiment had a yellow flag with a red lion under "МАКЕДОНЇЯ" (MAKEDONIJA, MACEDONIA). The flag has been lost and its design details are unknown (Матковски 1985).

The oldest Macedonian uprising flag is that of the Razlovci Uprising of 1876, created under the guidance of a teacher from Razlovci, Dimitar Pop Georgiev-Berovski (Fig. 6). On it a red lion appears, uncrowned and with one tail. That lion, together with the inscription "МАКЕДОНЇЯ" in an arc, is set on a gold rectangle shifted toward the hoist. The lion's appearance comes from Žefarović's *Stemmatographia* (among Georgiev-Berovski's personal effects were several attempts to draw the *Stemmatographia* lion). The flag was also used in the Macedonian (Kresna) Uprising of 1878 (Миљковиќ 2003, 23). With this, 117 years after the Ukrainian regiment, a flag with *a red lion on a gold field* bearing the inscription "МАКЕДОНЇЯ" again appeared as a military flag, and thus *de facto* became used specifically as a symbol of Macedonia.

After the failure of the Kresna Uprising, the Macedonian League was formed in 1880, with a formal headquarters. It defined both the coat of arms and the flag in Article 50 of its constitution: "The arms were *a red lion on a gold shield* crowned with a five-pointed crown. For all units, special flags were provided, red with a yellow lion, and the name of the unit under the arms." (Стојчев 2007, 53).

The aim of Macedonian independence advanced in 1893 with the formation of the Macedonian Revolutionary Organization (MRO). Its goals were to create an independent Macedonia and to protect the national identity of the Macedonian people. The methods of achieving these goals ranged from guerrilla warfare, through resistance, to a general uprising. The MRO's 1903 congress in Salonica initiated the Ilinden Uprising (Енциклопедија 2017, 126).

Flags had a central role during the Ilinden Uprising that August: each squad of *chetniks* (guerillas) had its own flag. Most often, the flag was embroidered on red silk. The rebellion's constitution defined the role of the flag, as well as the flag bearer and the permanent assistants responsible for guarding the flag.

Most of the Ilinden flags are preserved in Bulgaria and their study is based on recollections published in the *Ilinden* magazine, printed in Sofia. Unfortunately, while photographs of the revolutionary squads show many flag bearers with their flags, the content of the flags is barely recognizable (Миљковиќ 2003, 23). The flags were constructed from two separate pieces of fabric, often with different motifs on the obverse and reverse.

The flag of the village of Zagoričani in the Kostur region has a heraldic composition with *a red lion on a green field* (Fig. 7) in 3:4 proportions. Small white crescents are stitched in the corners, horns pointed outward. A tassel is sewn to each corner. (Иванов 1998, 43). On the obverse is *a red lion with one tail, crowned with a silver arched crown, its left paw holding a rifle in brown and silver and its right paw holding a silver sword.* "Свобода или смърть" (*Svoboda ili smrt*, Freedom or Death) is embroidered above the lion and in the lower part in small print is "20 юли 1903 г. Загоричани" (*20 juli 1903 g. Zagoričani*, 20 July 1903 Zagoričani). The date represents Ilinden, St. Elijah's Day—2 August in the Gregorian calendar. This flag covered the sarcophagus of the leader of the uprising, Goce Delčev, in the Ilinden House in Sofia; it was later surrendered to the Socialist Republic of Macedonia. The flag was most likely embroidered by Olga Hristova-Šatova, originally from Zagoričani. It was later presented to the squad of a warlord from Varna; its current whereabouts are unknown (Илустрација 1929).

The Kratovo flag has *a gold lion on a red field* (Fig. 8), 84 x 84 cm. The obverse bears a lion with one tail and no crown, painted in bronze on a red field. Above the lion in bronze is "KRATOVO", and below is "1903" (Иванов 1998, 50).

Figure 7 – Zagoričani flag

Figure 8 – Kratovo flag

In other flags, the lion is represented naturally (zoomorphically), not as a heraldic figure. Thus, on the Struga revolutionary flag embroidered in red silk, 100 x 80 cm, the red lion is not heraldic. The zoomorphic lion tramples a green Turkish flag with a white crescent and a star. The flag was produced in 1902 and took several months to embroider. The embroidery material was donated by three Struga teachers, members of the women's revolutionary organization in Struga: Slavka Čakarova-Puškareva, Careva Derebanova, and Anastasia Čakarova. The three teachers each gave some of their own hair to create the girl's hair on the flag (Струшкото 1925). On 23 July 1903, it was consecrated in Kuratičko, in the locality of Vilesloec, at the mountain headquarters in the presence of the units of Gorna and Dolna Debarca. The consecration was performed by Fr. Vasil, Naum Atanasov-Cvetanov, and Voyvoda (commander) Hristo Uzunov. All the revolutionaries passed by with caps in hand and kissed the flag (Кецкаровъ, 1936).

The Ohrid revolutionary flag bears two red lions in a non-heraldic composition (Fig. 9), 94 x 78 cm, embroidered on red silk. On the obverse is a girl in a white dress, holding a flag in her left hand bearing the text: "Свобода или смърть" (*Svoboda ili smrt*, Freedom or Death). Her image was influenced by *Marianne,* the French symbol of freedom. A lion, with one tail and no crown, stands with its front paws holding a flagstaff whose base stands on a small mosque; its hind legs stand on a red Turkish flag with a white crescent and a star. On the reverse of the flag is another red lion, with one tail and no crown, its front paws holding a gold crescent and a hind paw holding a gold star. The flag was designed by Ohrid artist Kliment Zarov-Čučučajkov and embroidered by teachers, Konstantina Bojadžieva-Nasteva, Klia Samardžieva, Atina Šakova, Aspasia Mileva, Katerina A. Kecakova, Poliksena Parmakovska, Poliksena Mosinova, and Anastasia Uzunova, along with other women.

Figure 9 – Ohrid revolutionary flag

The lion appears on six of the 16 Ilinden Uprising revolutionary flags for which we have information. Three depict the lion as a heraldic figure: on the red Razlovci flag *a red lion on a yellow field*; the Zagoričani flag (*a red lion on a green field*), and the Kratovo flag (*a gold lion on a red field*). On the other flags the lion is used as an emblem, but not in a heraldic position or in a heraldic composition; the colors of the lion are natural—embroidered with a dark red thread, while the mane is shown with a brighter thread.

* * *

The sun appears as part of the landscape for the first time on the Kumanovo flag, which differs by its iconography and design from other Ilinden flags (Fig. 10). This is the only original flag from the time of the Ilinden uprising preserved in Macedonia. It was displayed in the Assembly of the Municipality of Kumanovo until 1965 when it was transferred to the newly established Historical Museum in Kumanovo (Арсовски 1986).

In the middle of the obverse is a panel showing a rebel in a brown robe holding a rifle and a bayonet in his right hand and the staff of a red flag in his left hand, arrayed against a landscape of sunrise and mountains. Above the image is inscribed "ИЛИНДЕНЬ" (ILINDEN) and "Свобода или смърть" (*Sloboda ili smrt*, Freedom or death), and "1903".

On the reverse is inscribed "ОСВОБОДЕНА МАКЕДОНИЯ" (*OSVOBODENA MAKEDONIJA*, MACEDONIA FREED) and "КУМАНОВО" (KUMANOVO). In the middle is a panel showing a girl in a folk costume and with broken ties on her hands. On each leg is a ball and chain and the background is a landscape with sunrise and mountains (Миљковиќ, 23). The Kumanovo flag depicts the sun as part of the landscape, a sunrise which would prevail as a concept in the next era. The sunrise, representing a new birth, became a symbol of the goal of the revolution—freedom.

Figure 10 – Kumanovo flag

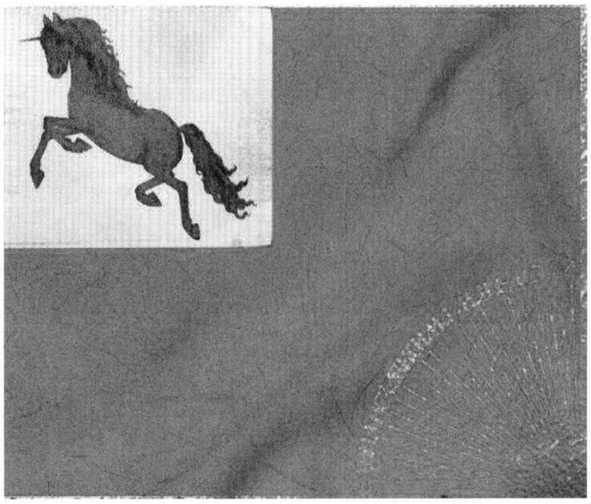

Figure 11 – Flag of Macedonia proposed by the St. Petersburg colony

The proposal of the Macedonian colony in St. Petersburg, Russia, for the flag of Macedonia is of particular importance among the civil flags of the Macedonian national movement (Fig. 11). This Macedonian scientific-literary comradeship, which operated in St. Petersburg under various names from 1902 to 1917 under the leadership of Dimitrija Čupovski, was committed to a unique Macedonian nationality and statehood (cf. Ристовски 1978). The journal *Makedonskiy Golos* published the flag in 1914, as an illustration titled "Macedonian Flag" without any explanation or accompanying text (*Македонскій* 1914).

The flag is red with a white canton, in which there is a red unicorn (despite having been perceived as Alexander's horse Bucephalus). In the lower fly corner there is a quarter-sun in gold with many rays depicted as narrow gold lines, around which runs the inscription in decorative oblique letters in gold: "Едина независима Македония" (*Edina Nezavisima Makedonija*, One Independent Macedonia).

The sunrise represents the rise of long-awaited freedom. This flag was the first official flag proposal that sought to represent or symbolize an independent Macedonia. The flag was brought to Macedonia by Academician Blaže Ristovski, donated by Velko Jonovski, and is now exhibited in the Museum of Macedonia (Ристовски 1978, 291).

2.   The Sun and the Lion in the Arms and Flags of Macedonia after 1944

The Yugoslav Federation, which included Macedonia as one of six constituent republics, emerged out of the National Liberation War (NLW) during the Second World War under the leadership of Marshal Josip Broz Tito. It was declared to be a community of equal peoples and nationalities, best shown by the slogan "brotherhood—unity."

The joint struggle was presented as the century-long aspiration of "our peoples" (based on Slavism as a connecting element) for national and class freedom, in which the anti-fascist struggle was the last phase. In this sense, through the NLW as the last and complete phase of that struggle, the Macedonian people crowned their long-standing fight for their own country with their own individuality. However, the ancient pre-Slavic Macedonian identity was suppressed as inconsistent with the Pan-Slavism which served as the unifying element for Yugoslavia (which means "South Slavic").

The first symbol of the ideology of socialism and communism is the plain red flag, which probably originated from the *baucans*, the red naval pennant which in the Middle Ages symbolized a struggle to the last. When used by the Paris Commune in 1871, it became a symbol of socialism and communism. Another important symbol of communism is the red star, whose five points represent the five fingers of the worker's hand and the five continents on which communism would prevail.

After the 1917 October Revolution in Russia, a new concept of state symbols emerged emphasizing the new socialist ideology above all. The sun as a symbol of the new beginning—a new, different, better world—appeared on the emblems of the new state, the Soviet Union, and its republics. In their insignias (officially called "coat of arms"), the common contents were the wheat wreath, the ribbon, the five-pointed star, and the hammer and sickle. This concept, so-called "socialist heraldry," departed deliberately from traditional heraldry, which the Communists regarded as a legacy of feudalism.

In Macedonia, the struggle for its people's freedom was, in fact, a struggle for two kinds of freedoms: national and class. Both were desired and intertwined, but also in some ways replaced, supplemented, and sometimes opposed. These struggles would inspire the selection of Macedonian symbols.

Class freedom in Macedonia was advanced by socialist ideas starting in 1894, when Vasil Glavinov established the first workers' cultural education society in Veles. In 1898 Macedonian Socialists started the newspaper *Политическа свобода* [*Political Freedom*] to promote the struggle for the liberation of the Macedonian people and the spread of socialist ideas, believing that without national liberation there would be no economic freedom (Револю́ция 1895, 1).

With the Balkan wars of 1912–13, the territory of Macedonia was divided into three parts, a condition that continued after the First World War. The part that today comprises the Republic of Macedonia was incorporated into the Kingdom of the Serbs, Croats, and Slovenes (later Yugoslavia). This discussion focuses precisely on this part, the territory that is today the Republic of Macedonia.

The sun as a symbol announces freedom. The sunrise—the dawn, which is present on the Kumanovo Ilinden flag and the flag for Macedonia created in St. Petersburg—continues to be an inspirational symbol of freedom. It is also referred to in song, such as in *The March of the*

Macedonian Revolutionaries, composed in 1918, commonly known by its first stanza "The dawn of freedom" (Младеновски 2004, 27).[29] The march, as sung in the period between the two world wars, functioned as a Macedonian anthem.[30]

Figure 12 – Proposed coat of arms for Skopje, 1928

Figure 13 – Reconstruction of the coat of arms of Skopje, 1941

The Dawn of Freedom is a revolutionary march and has many class elements emphasizing the eternal struggle of all workers of the world, similar to the lyrics of *The Internationale*. The text glorifies heroism; Macedonia is mentioned only once. It uses the dawn as a symbol of both class and national freedom. The sunrise symbolizes the change of state, from night to day, from darkness to light, from slavery to freedom.

The sun is also found in an armorial composition of the city of Skopje dating from 21 February 1928, which is supposed to be a proposal for arms (Fig. 12). In the heraldic composition, on the shield is the Stone Bridge, under which flows the River Vardar, as well as a landscape behind the bridge with mountain and fort. Behind the mountain, the sun rises behind the clouds in an artistic interpretation that cannot be blazoned. Behind the shield is a large mantle with a crown.[31] The current arms (designed in the 1930s) uses a shield with similar content but without the sun.

The lion as symbol in municipal heraldry appears only once, on the coat of arms of the city of Skopje during the Bulgarian occupation during the Second World War (Fig. 13). Mayor Janko Mustafov, on 12 July 1941, announced the coat of arms of Skopje as: "City Fortress, a lion holding a flag, a wheat stalk, the Šara mountain and the bridge over the river Vardar, as well as the motto 'Shine and live well'" (Протокол 1941). (The Ministry of Internal Affairs and

---

[29] The authorship of the text and the melody is attributed to the composer Alexander Vasilev Morfov (1880–1934), born in Plovdiv (*Песни на българското работническо движение 1891–1944.* Съставител Никола Кауфман. Българска академия на науките, Институт за музика, София, 1959, 495).

[30] The anthem is performed on important events from the political, but also cultural and sports life, such as public holidays, festivals, international sports events, etc., which are often prescribed by law.

[31] The nonheraldic composition of 1928 also has the coat of arms of the Kingdom of Serbs, Croats, and Slovenes placed over the top of the shield. The image is black and white and the author's name is signed on it: probably "сл. Ђ. Сутулаћ" [Đ. Sutulać].

People's Health from Sofia changed the red flag displayed by the lion to the Bulgarian tricolor.) After liberation, Skopje returned to a pre-war coat of arms without a lion or sun.

2.1. The Sun and the Lion in the Arms, Flag, and Anthem in the "Yugoslav" context

Macedonia achieved sovereignty within Yugoslavia through the Anti-Fascist Assembly of the People's Liberation of Macedonia (ASNOM) as a "solution to the Macedonian national question." ASNOM, often referred to as the "Second Ilinden," was held on 2 August 1944, the 41st anniversary of the Ilinden Uprising. In the Yugoslav Federation, the main ideology was the "brotherhood and unity" of all the constituent peoples who won their freedom through joint struggle during the NLW under the leadership of Marshal Tito. While Macedonian identity was "hidden" behind the collective Yugoslav identity, it was recognized through the perception of the Ilinden Uprising as the foundation of the Macedonian struggle for national and social freedom, conceived as an advanced socialist movement that shaped the "first republic in the Balkans," headed by the socialist Nikola Karev. The last stage of this struggle was the NLW, during which the goal was achieved. The two Ilindens were perceived as special events connected in single story (Поповска, 2015, 39).

During the NLW and the Socialist Revolution, certain symbolic elements were selected as important and placed on the coat of arms and the flag of Macedonia within the Yugoslav Federation. During this period, two interconnected concepts found reflection in the design of the symbols of the Macedonian state: 1) national and social liberation and 2) the idea of unifying Macedonia. Shortly before the outbreak of the Second World War, the Provincial Committee of the Communist Party of Yugoslavia in Macedonia formulated the basic elements of the national program as "total liberation and equality." Macedonia was understood to have ethnic and geographic borders (the entire region of Macedonia), with Vardar Macedonia as the center for unification and creation of an independent Macedonian state (Историја 2008, 263).

The unification of Macedonia became the primary goal of the national liberation movement, which had an emotional charge and romantic appeal. It was intertwined with the ideas of proletarian internationalism and a cosmopolitan approach. ASNOM proclaimed the idea of unification with the demand for unification of the entire Macedonian people under the principles of self-determination. That desire was clearly expressed at the First ASNOM Session and through the ASNOM Manifesto. The Macedonian leadership believed that the unification of the three parts of Macedonia would be a condition for lasting peace in the Balkans.

The creation of the free territory in Macedonia in 1943 enabled the people's government and socio-political, cultural, and religious life to function. On the basis of the decisions of the Second Session of Antifascist Assembly of the People's Liberation of Yugoslavia (AVNOJ), for the first time the Macedonian people gained the opportunity to continue the struggle for the creation of their own Macedonian state as an equal member of the Yugoslav Federation. The sun became part of the official culture thanks to the advancement of ideas related to the achievement of long-awaited freedom, which the sun the embodied as a symbol.

2.2. The Arms and Flag of the People's / Socialist Republic of Macedonia

The basis of the design of the Macedonian flag emerged from the Conference of the General Headquarters of the National Liberation Partisan Units of Yugoslavia in Stolice in 1941. This laid the foundations of the partisan units of Yugoslavia, creating the basis for the future state union with Macedonia as a constituent part (Билтен 1941a). Partisan units were defined as combat units of the peoples of Yugoslavia, and an advisory order defined the red five-pointed star, together with the national flag, as their distinguishing mark. This order used the general concept of military designation—a national flag plus a red five-pointed star that would become part of the new concept of national flags of the federal republics in the Federation. In this order, Macedonia and its flag were not mentioned, but this concept was later reflected during the design of the Macedonian flag (Билтен 1941b).

In the summer of 1942, the design of the Macedonian flag was discussed for the first time at the meeting of the General Staff of the Peoples' Liberation Partisan Units of Macedonia (PUM), when the commander, Mihajlo Apostolski, was preparing to go into battle leading the partisan units. He said: "Partisan units should fly a flag. And what will be the flag?" After analyzing the flags of the Ilinden Uprising of 1903, a red flag was chosen (Солунски 1993, 102).

Two flags used during the Ilinden Uprising had socialist symbolism. The first, a red flag proper, with no additional symbols, could be considered a flag of the uprising as distinct from that of the MRO organization: "... above the town of Kruševo was the red flag proper instead of that black-and-white flag with a skull and crossed bones, which was a symbol of the uprising." (Pribichevich 1982, 128; Laqueur 2009, 182).

The second, the flag of the Krushevo squad, differed from all other revolutionary flags that included socialist rather than national symbols. In the middle of a red field, embroidered with a yellow silk thread, appear two hands shaking over a palm wreath, and a torch above the hands. Around them is the inscription "Смърть или свобода—Знаме на Крушовската чета" (*Smrt ili Svoboda—zname na Krushovskata cheta,* Death or Freedom—Flag of the Krushevo Squad). (Илустрация 1935).

In accordance with the provisions for partisan flags in the advisory order in Stolice, the Macedonian flag bore a red five-pointed star in the center, bordered in yellow-gold (Солунски 1993, 102). At the partisan base at the main headquarters of PUM (Partisan Units in Macedonia) in Lopušnik, Kičevo, the appearance of the Macedonian flag was similarly determined—a red field with the same red five-pointed star, but with yellow edges (Младеновски 2004, 24). This design, inscribed with names of military units, became a template for military flags. However, sometimes the star was in the canton, as seen a photograph from Kičevo in March 1943.

The first mention of a flag in official documents is in the proclamation to the Macedonian people of 19 November 1944. In it the term *flag* is mentioned twice. First, "the red Macedonian flag is flown high" over the liberated territory, then a few paragraphs later: "Bring the red partisan flag as soon as possible in our native Skopje, fly it high above its mountain."[32]

This suggests that in the hierarchy of symbols, the red flag was at the highest position, and it became the basis on which other possible symbols were placed, such as, for example, a five-pointed star or something else. The red flag was perceived as both Macedonian and Partisan. This stems from the fact that the Macedonian flag and the flags of other Yugoslav republics were

---

[32] Presidium of ASNOM, session held in the village of Gorno Vranovci on 19 September 1944.

first military flags and then transformed into the state symbols of the national republics. This also shows how dual symbolism can persist at the same time. On the one hand, the Macedonian flag was connected with the flag of the Kruševo Republic (mentioned in the anthem *Today over Macedonia*) as a symbol of the 100-year struggle for freedom, but also as a symbol of the partisan movement in the NLW, the last and most important stage of that struggle. Therefore, leaders urged that the flag be taken to the capital of Skopje, as a symbol of the final victory and final liberation of Macedonia.

The red flag with a five-pointed star was perceived as national, of course, according to the ideological context of that time. During this period, the flag of the USSR was popular in Yugoslavia and Macedonia as a flag of an ally in both national and class liberation. The popular flag of the Communist Party of Yugoslavia had a similar design: a red flag with a red five-pointed star in the canton, edged in gold, bearing a crossed hammer and sickle. In the upper part of the flag is written the slogan "Пролетери свих земаља уједините се" (*Proleteri svih zemalja ujedinite se*, Workers from all countries unite).

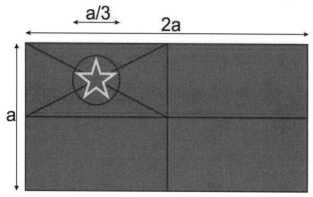

Figure 14 – Construction of the flag of the People's Republic of Macedonia

The flag of the People's Republic of Macedonia was established in Article 4 of its first constitution of 31 December 1946 (Службен 1947). It is red in proportions of 1:2. On it is a red five-pointed star in the canton, distinguished from the field by a yellow fimbriation (Fig. 14). According to the 1974 law, the diameter of implied circle enclosing the star is 0.33 of the height of the flag, smaller than on the tricolor of the Yugoslavia, and of the republics of Serbia, Croatia, Montenegro, and Slovenia, where it is 0.6 of the height of the flag.

* * *

Figure 15 – Arms of the People's Republic of Macedonia, 1946

After the Second World War, Eastern bloc countries adopted the Soviet style of state symbolism. Thus the rising sun could be found on the state emblems of several socialist countries.

The coat of arms of the People's Republic of Macedonia was a purely landscape composition, with the sun rising behind the central element, a mountain (Fig. 15). Vasilije Popović-Cico created the artwork; his interpretation of the design of the emblem appeared six month later, slightly altered, in the first constitution adopted 31 December 1946.

The use of different versions of the coat of arms can be traced through its presence on the cover of the *Official Gazette of the Federal Unit of Macedonia*. The Presidium of ASNOM established the *Official Gazette* on 18 February 1945 as the official newsletter of the Macedonian state—"Federal Unit Macedonia in Democratic and Federal Yugoslavia." The release began on 23 February 1945, with the publication of the second issue. This and the next issue of April

1945 were published without a coat of arms on the front page. From number 5 (3 May 1945), until the adoption of the Law on the Coat of Arms of the People's Republic of Macedonia, number 24 (30 July 1946), the *Official Gazette* carried the coat of arms of Democratic Federal Yugoslavia.

"The Coat of Arms of the People's Republic of Macedonia" was adopted as the first item on the agenda of the Second Extraordinary Session of the National Assembly, held in Skopje on 26 July 1946. The draft bill was presented by people's delegate Dimče Belovski, and the debate was attended by people's delegate Dr. Blagoj Arsov and the Minister of Education Nikola Minčev, after which the Law was accepted unanimously (Народното 1946).

The Law on the Coat of Arms of the People's Republic of Macedonia, in Article 1, describes this coat of arms.

> The coat of arms of the People's Republic of Macedonia is a field surrounded by wheat stalks intertwined with poppy fruits and tobacco leaves, which at the bottom are connected with a ribbon embroidered with folk motifs. On the ribbon is written "N. R. Macedonia."[33] At the top is a five-pointed star. In the middle of the field is a mountain; a river flows at its foot. Behind the mountain the sun rises (Закон за грб 1946).

Two days later the newspaper *Nova Makedonija*, the organ of the People's Front of Macedonia functioning as an official journal, published this law together with an image of the coat of arms and an explanation.

> The coat of arms of the People's Republic of Macedonia is a symbol of freedom and brotherhood of the Macedonian people and the wealth of the Macedonian land. The wheat stalks, poppy fruits, and tobacco leaves represent the wealth of Macedonia and the diversity of its economy. The five-pointed star symbolizes the national liberation war with which the Macedonian people won freedom. The national motif on the ribbon expresses the richness and beauty of the national essence. In the middle of the field is Mount Pirin, the largest in Macedonian and the center of the People's Liberation Wars in the past, and the river that flows is the river Vardar, the most famous Macedonian river in the Republic. Pirin and Vardar simultaneously represent the unity of all parts of Macedonia and the ideal of our people for national unification. The sun represents the free and creative life in Macedonia (Народното 1946).

From this description, we learn the arms are a symbol of freedom, fraternity, and the wealth of the Macedonian land. The five-pointed star is a symbol of the National Liberation War (as a means of gaining freedom rather than a symbol of Communist ideology). Among the main internal elements, the mountain and the river represent the Pirin and Vardar (and Aegean) parts of Macedonia (the river Vardar flows into the Aegean Sea, representing the Aegean part of Macedonia). The two elements together represent the "unity of all parts of Macedonia and the ideal of our people for national unification." Their obvious message is the ideal of national unification, which was still alive at that time, especially with the idea of a Balkan federal republic proposed by Josip Broz Tito and Georgi Dimitrov to unite Yugoslavia and Bulgaria, which would have merged Vardar with Pirin Macedonia.

The sun, the final element, symbolizes freedom and creativity. It meant that now the people could freely declare themselves Macedonian in every respect—everything that appears as

---

[33] N(arodna) R(epublika) – Peoples Republic.

a creation, as a culture, gets the epithet Macedonian. Simply put, the Macedonian could for the first time be freely identified as Macedonian. In the previous period, these elements of culture, work, propaganda machineries, and political communities where the Macedonian persisted were interpreted as Serbian, Bulgarian, or Greek. The symbolism coincides fully with the meaning of the texts of the two anthems—the sun of freedom. The elements collectively symbolize the liberation and unification of the material and spiritually rich Macedonia through the National Liberation War.

This Law was published in the *Official Gazette* number 24 (30 June 1946). The coat of arms of Democratic Federal Yugoslavia appeared on the cover of the number, which included the text of the Law along with an image of the arms—they graced the next issue, number 25 (10 August 1946).

Figure 16 – Arms of the People's Republic of Macedonia from the exhibition of works of Vasilije Popović-Cico

While the colors were not described or depicted, they could be seen 68 years later in an exhibition of Popović-Cico's works in Skopje on 4 December 2014 (Fig. 16). The field is light blue; the sun, the poppy flowers and wheat stalks are yellow; the tobacco leaves are green with white flowers; the base under the mountain has blue wavy lines. The five-pointed star is red and the ribbon is red with white with "N. R. Macedonia" in black letters.

The arms began to be used in public and also in homes, appearing on a 1947 calendar published in the newspaper *Nova Makedonija* on 29 December 1946 (Fig. 17). In it the arms have a slightly different design. The sun is represented by 13 visible rays that emerge from the sun and spread beyond the arms throughout the calendar (Календар за 1947).

Nova Makedonija gave no details about the authorship or meaning of the arms. But usually such discussions would not go into the details of the law itself, but rather would glorify the benefits of the NLW and the revolution. For example, for a series of other laws, it mentions that the constitution is written "with the blood of young partisans" (Вчера 1946).

Article 3 of the proposed constitution of the People's Republic of Macedonia, published as a supplement in *Nova Makedonija*, described the arms.

Figure 17 – Calendar for 1947

The State Coat of Arms of the People's Republic of Macedonia represents a field surrounded by wheat stalks, intertwined with poppy fruits and tobacco leaves, which are connected to the bottom with a ribbon embroidered with folk motifs. The ribbon is inscribed "The People's Republic of Macedonia." Between the tops of the stalks is a five-pointed star. In the middle of the field there is a silhouette of a mountain, at the foot of which a river flows. Beyond the mountain the sun rises. (Проект на Устав 1946).

This differs from the description in the Law on the Coat of Arms—the proposal uses "The People's Republic of Macedonia" in the text of the ribbon rather than "N.R. Macedonia." However, the ribbon's text is omitted entirely from Article 3 of the first constitution of the People's Republic of Macedonia (Устав 1946). Neither description mentions colors. The wax seal attached to the constitution contains the new design of the arms, which appeared in the *Official Gazette* number 17 (23 April 1947), with a design combining the old and new arms. Beginning with number 26 (6 August 1947), the new design of the arms appeared, with an elliptical instead of circular field. This design would be used for the next 62 years.

Heraldic and graphic analysis

The emblem of the People's Republic of Macedonia was not designed according to heraldic principles and therefore is not a heraldic coat of arms, although it may be analyzed using heraldic concepts. According to the official description, the emblem is a field surrounded by a wreath. Therefore, as a small coat of arms, the field may be considered as a shield, while all elements that are not completely on the oval shield may be considered external ornaments.

The shield is oval, one of the heraldic types of shield. The shield's blazon should contain the colors of the fields. The official description does not contain a definition of colors, but we can attempt to blazon the colorful version with natural colors on Popović-Cico's 1946 arms (Joновски 2015, 157).

The shield is undoubtedly blue celeste and its main figure is the gold rising sun of the socialist or linear type. The mountain is very small, and may be regarded as a base in the form of a mountain. Water is represented at the foot of the mountain with very narrow wavy lines.

The heraldic blazon of such a composition would be: *Bleu celeste, a rising sun proper, a mount Azure issuing from waves Argent*. The shape of the shield does not blazon. If the shape is essential, then the description (not the blazon) would be: *on an oval shield bleu celeste, a gold (linear) sun rising, blue mount in the base issuing from silver waves*. The use of small arms represents the "Slovenian solution" as the simplest design for heraldic arms.

A wreath of wheat connected at the bottom with a ribbon is not unknown in classical heraldry, but not one that surrounds a circular or oval field. These details, together with the red five-pointed star, demonstrate its socialist design.

Figure 18 – Comparison of the construction of the arms in 1946 and 1947

In later versions of the arms, the relationship and distribution of the elements in the field changed (Fig. 18). The mountain on the 1946 arms is 1/4 of the height of the field, on the 1947 arms it is 5/8 of the height of the field (its *area* increased by 2/3). The solar disk is reduced slightly in diameter, but raised so that its upper edge moved from 1/3 to 2/3 of the height of the field. The ratio of the diameter of the sun and the field is approximately 1:2.

In the first design of the coat of arms of the People's Republic of Macedonia the mountain and the solar disk are set very low, giving the impression of room left for another element. The height of the sun was the same as on Serbia's coat of arms, supporting a theory that it left space for the land arms of Macedonia. According to Niko Tozija, who helped design the arms, Popović-Cico was aware of the traditional coat of arms of Macedonia, but did not use it in the design (Грбовите на Македонија). Popović-Cico probably could have learned of the traditional arms, *a red lion on gold field*, only from Žefarović's *Stemmatographia* or sources from the 18th or 19th centuries, which are mostly based on Žefarović. The *gold lion on red field* (colors reversed) would be promoted by Aleksandar Matkovski as the sole Macedonian coat of arms just 24 years later.[34]

A more recent theory holds that Popović-Cico knew of the 16-rayed sun and secretly included it in the arms of the People's Republic of Macedonia. This theory is based on how eight rays are visible on the arms, leaving eight more rays in the part that is not visible. One possible interpretation of the reason for this is that the "sun over Macedonia is only partly the sun of freedom since only Vardar Macedonia is liberated; because of that there are eight rays, and not 16 like the true Macedonian sun."[35]

However, an extrapolation from the number of visible rays in the 1946 arms shows that the sun has 31 rays in total. In the 1947 arms, depending on the extrapolation method, the sun has 17 or 18 rays (Fig. 19). In no case is a 16-rayed sun hidden in the arms (Јоновски 2015, 168). However, the issue is not the number of rays, the essential difference is in the design of the sun, changing from a socialist version to the Kutleš (Vergina) type.

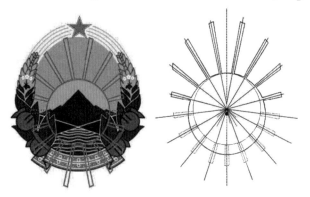

Figure 19 – Construction of the number of rays according two methods

The central element of the Macedonian coat of arms has actually been the mountain (which also appears on the arms of the People's Republics of Slovenia, Bosnia and Herzegovina, and Montenegro—all those that did not retain their historical arms). The Law's description of the arms states that "[i]n the field there is a silhouette of a mountain, at the foot of which a river flows. Beyond the mountain the sun rises." The sun is described last, as a routine part of socialist heraldry along with a wreath of wheat with a ribbon and a red five-pointed star.

Neither the constitution nor any other law provided specifications for the arms of Macedonia, resulting in many variants—differing mostly in the size of the five-pointed star—which often surface when the arms are printed, embroidered, or stylized on other materials. Each institution has its own version of the graphic design.

---

[34] Matkovski himself claims that before the 1960s, nobody knew about the gold lion on a red background like the land arms. In the collection of personal items he left to a museum, the oldest correspondence with colleagues from abroad is from 1966, from Sofia, but the name can not be read from the envelope. Архив на МАНУ, фонд „Александар Матковски." АЕ 63/I/1.

[35] Similar statements have been expressed many times. For an example see https://www.erepublik.com/it/**article**/-1-2232026/1/20, accessed on 26.6.2017.

2.3. The Interest and Popularization of the Lion in the Socialist Republic of Macedonia

Figure 20– *Žurnal* magazine, 1969

The first mention since early in the century of the lion as an emblem on the coat of arms of Macedonia appeared in a 1966 article by Stjepan Antoljak in *Auxiliary Historical Sciences*, which called it the "fictitious coat of arms of Macedonia" and cited two sources: the Fojnica Armorial with a *gold lion on red* and the *Stemmatographia* of Vitezović, with a *red lion on gold* (Антољак 1966, 276). Then in 1968 Aleksandar Matkovski promoted Illyrian heraldry and the Macedonian arms of a *gold lion on red* on Radio-Television Skopje's show "The Living Being—the Word", hosted by Academician Blaže Ristovski (Стенографски 1992, IX / 8).

In 1969 the magazine *Žurnal* published an issue dedicated to "the Macedonian coat of arms from 1340" (Fig. 20), dated 11 October (the day of the People's Uprising in the Second World War). The unattributed text described the Macedonian coat of arms from the Fojnica Armorial that "later appeared throughout the Turkish period, on various occasions, and always retained the same symbol—*a gold crowned lion on red field.*" The issue also showed the coats of arms of other Southern Slavic countries, along with the "Common Coat of Arms of the Southern Slavic Peoples" (Македонскиот грб 1968, 23). Matkovski believed that the author to be Dr. Slavko Dimovski, who in other articles "bragged that he discovered the Macedonian coat of arms from 1340" (Матковски 1968).

That same year, in the journal *History*, Aleksandar Matkovski published "The oldest coat of arms of Macedonia," without using the term "Land." His paper identified Peter Ohmučević as the author of the coat of arms, mentioning the purported protoarmorial preceding the 1595 armorial of Korenić-Neorić (Матковски 1969). The next year his *The Coats of Arms of Macedonia: Appendix to Macedonian Heraldry* (Матковски, 1970) advanced the theory that the Macedonian "land" coat of arms was *a gold crowned lion on red.* While he mentioned the existence of a series of coats of arms with *red lion on gold*, he considered them merely an "error" by Vitezović. The book, edited by Academician Blaže Ristovski, was published by the Institute of National History and the daily newspaper *Nova Makedonija*.[36]

Matkovski's book popularized the concept of the lion as a symbol of Macedonia and shared the image of the actual coat of arms from the armorials (which, located in libraries, archives, and monasteries would otherwise not have been available).

These efforts attempted to promote the theme of heraldry and the arms with the lion in the public sphere. Although they had little effect domestically, the symbolism caught on among political emigrants in the Macedonian diaspora.

---

[36] The book is 17 x 24 cm; so far we found two hardcover and two softcover editions. It has 219 pages, of which ten are in German and ten in English.

2.4. The Sun and the Lion as Symbols in the Macedonian Diaspora

Figure 21 – The lion on the flag, *United Macedonia* masthead, 1975

Disagreement about the status of Macedonia within the Yugoslav Federation (where it comprised only part of its historical territory) as well as disagreement with communist ideology led to extensive political emigration after the Second World War. Advocates for an independent and united Macedonian state created conspiracy groups, many with "VMRO" (Internal Macedonian Revolutionary Organization) in their names (Тодоровски 2000, 43); most were discovered and their members arrested and imprisoned (Миноски 1993).

After the Greek Civil War (1947–1949) and the atrocities inflicted on Macedonia's civilian population, political conditions, and economic difficulties spurred the emigration of Macedonians from the Vardar, Pirin, and especially Aegean parts of Macedonia. They emigrated to Canada, the United States, and Australia, as well as to Western European countries, and advanced the Macedonian national movement among the members of the diaspora (Томов 2012a). The symbols of the sun and the lion developed there, "returning" to Macedonia in the late 1980s.

Beginning in 1956, nationalist and activist Dragan Bogdanovski organized a number of Macedonian organizations in Europe. The Liberation Committee of Macedonia (OKM) was founded in 1962 in Trelleborg, Sweden; in 1973 it became the Movement for Liberation and Reunion of Macedonia (DOOM). The journal *Македонска нација* [*Macedonian Nation*] became the official organ of DOOM (Иваноски 2015, 344). Bogdanovski would eventually be imprisoned.

The lion appeared as a symbol of the Macedonian diaspora in the logo of the newspaper *Обединета Македонија* [*United Macedonia*], published by DOOM in Munich in 1975 (Fig. 21). The left part of the masthead showed a red flag with a white heraldic lion, with no crown and a single tail, above it the text "Macedonia" in white. The lion image did not come from any of the Macedonian arms published by Matkovski, but was likely an available generic design. A flag with the same design would later be flown at the founding assembly of VMRO-DPMNE (Internal Macedonian Revolutionary Organization—Democratic Party for Macedonian National Unity) in Skopje in 1990.

Figure 22– Logo of DOOM, 1975 **Figure 23 – Mike Apostolov stamp, 1976** **Figure 24 – Stamp of NOFM, 1984**

The lion appeared on the logo of DOOM itself, as seen in the first "pirate" issue of the newspaper *Macedonian Nation* from 1976 (Fig. 22). The logo has a map of ethnic Macedonia and a lion (with a saber and a rifle, taken from the Zagoričani flag). A coat of arms with the lion also appears on the seal of Mike Apostolov (the vice president of DOOM in the United States), imprinted on a letter he sent to the journal *Macedonian Nation* on 1 January 1976 (Fig. 23). Whether it is a personal or organizational seal, it shows that among the diaspora the lion was perceived as a symbol of Macedonia, and therefore of Macedonians (Апостолов 1976). In 1984, when the organization was consolidated and renamed the National Liberation Front of Macedonia (NOFM), its seal again showed arms bearing a lion with a linear-type sun above, surrounded by a floral wreath (Fig. 24) (Богдановски 1989).[37]

Political conditions in the Socialist Republic of Macedonia began to change in 1988, signaled by the large number of Macedonian immigrants arriving for the traditional gathering of "Children Refugees" (from Aegean Macedonia during the Greek Civil War of 1947–49) in the village of Trnovo, Bitola (Томов 2012b). After serving his prison sentence, Dragan Bogdanovski connected with a small number of Macedonians during a stay in Skopje. From that 1988 meeting the VMRO-DPMNE party would emerge and take as its logo the lion from the land coats of arms of Macedonia.

The use of the sun and the lion as symbols in the Macedonian diaspora can be followed by analyzing the symbols used in the mastheads of its newspapers and other printed material. An examination of the titles published in the *Macedonian Emigrant Press*, including 49 newspapers from Australia, 66 from North America, and 17 from Europe, shows that most newspapers had a masthead without additional illustration (Николовски 1993). But among the illustrated mastheads, the lion appeared five times and the sun 12 times.

The first sun, of the linear type, appeared as part of the logo of "United Macedonians" in the *Ilinden* newspaper of Toronto in 1961, and in the logo of the *Macedonian Truth* in Melbourne in 1970. In Australia, the first lion (derived from the Macedonian land arms in the Bologna Armorial of 1689) appeared on the cover of the newspaper *Macedonia—Weekly Messenger*, in Melbourne in 1982.

Of the newspapers in Australia, 19 mastheads were illustrated: two with linear suns, two with the land coat of arms, and one with a lion in combination with the symbol of Vardar,

---

[37] This version of the shield, with its indented shape and spiky crown, seems derived from the image in the Fojnica Armorial.

Aegean, and Pirin Macedonia—three torches bearing the letters V, E, and P. On the North American continent, 29 mastheads were illustrated, most frequently with the logo of the United Macedonians (on nine newspapers). That symbol combined a small linear sun with two hands shaking, with the Canadian maple leaf with the three-torch VEP symbol on a closed book with the letter "M" around which the sun shines. One instance in 1974 had a lion and a convergent sun with 16 rays. Of nine European newspapers with illustrated mastheads, the lion appeared on one, and the sun did not appear at all.

These symbols were not just "ordinary" logos of newspapers, but symbols that the Macedonian emigration perceived as their own, as Macedonian.

Figure 25 – The Soviet-style emblem of the Socialist Republic of Macedonia, officially called the Coat of Arms (1970)

3.   The Sun and the Lion on the Macedonian Coat of Arms and Flag after 1991

Independence in 1991 found Macedonia unprepared "symbolically" and "emblematically". The People's Republic / Socialist Republic of Macedonia had used three symbols for 40 years: the star from the flag, the mountain, and the sun from the state emblem (Fig. 25).[38] Then during the last decade of the 20th century two symbols previously used by the Macedonian diaspora—the gold lion and the gold 16-rayed sun on a red field—were slowly introduced to the public inside Macedonia. An example of this would be the rally in Skopje for the proclamation of the results of the Referendum on 8 September 1991 (Референдум во Македонија 1991).

After Tito's death in 1980, Yugoslavia slowly but surely collapsed. As it did, Macedonia had two options—remain a part of Yugoslavia or seize the opportunity to achieve the "centuries-old dream of an independent state" (Тошевски 2011, 18).

The processes that led to the independence of the states emerging from the Yugoslav Federation also led to "new" symbols for them. The choice and development of the symbols which would come to represent the new states began in the diasporas. For example, the Serbian and Croatian diasporas had strongly opposed Socialist Yugoslavia and actively worked against the Federation, including armed incidents in the country and abroad. Their symbols were considered nationalistic and anti-Yugoslavian.

The Macedonian diaspora primarily advocated the liberation and unification of ethnic Macedonia. It directed its activity toward supporting the Macedonians in Greece, where they lacked basic human rights such as using their language, as well as those expelled from the Aegean part of Macedonia. Also Macedonians born in Greece and expelled did not have the right to visit their relatives or the homes and graveyards of their ancestors. Discussion of the so-called "Macedonian Question" in the relations of Yugoslavia with Greece had long been suppressed. With the loosening of relations within the Federation in 1988 came the first public

---

[38] The Law describing the People's Republic of Macedonia's arms refers to a mountain shape in the field and, at the end, mentions the rising sun.

and unauthorized rallies against Greece's negative attitude towards Macedonia and the Macedonians, especially those living in the Aegean part of Macedonia (in Greece).

This coincided with Greece's decision to rename its Ministry of Northern Greece as the Ministry of Macedonia and Thrace, a change from its previous position—denying the existence of Macedonia—to asserting that Macedonia had always been and was only Greek.

At these protests, red flags were flown with a gold lion in a design like the one on the *United Macedonia* masthead and (for the first time) with a gold 16-rayed sun (*Exclusive* 1988). The same flags were used by the Macedonian diaspora in Australia, America, and Europe, and were flown in protests in Australia and America on 25 February 1988 (*Macedonian* 1988), as well as in Melbourne on 26 November 1989 (*Ethnic* 1989) and in Toronto on 25 March 1990 (*Macedonian* 1990).

Such protests, in support of the Macedonians in Greece and against Greece's chauvinist policy, took place in Skopje, first on 23 November 1988 in front of the Greek Consulate (*First* 1988) and in February 1990 in the city square. In videos of these protests only the flags of Yugoslavia and the Socialist Republic of Macedonia can be seen—no flags with the lion or the 16-rayed sun (*Macedonian* 1990b). The use of flags with the lion would become dominant in Macedonia after the republication of Matkovski's *The Coats of Arms of Macedonia* in 1990.

* * *

The sun as a millennia-old symbol of Macedonia gained stronger symbolic meaning after the discovery of the royal tomb in Vergina (*Kutleš* in Slavic) in 1977. In it a sarcophagus, presumably that of King Philip II of Macedonia, was found, bearing a distinctive sun image.[39] As the sarcophagus had no colors, when the Macedonian diaspora began to fly a flag with that Vergina/Kutleš sun image in the late 1980s, it used the current national flag's colors of gold and red.[40] That flag first flew in public in Macedonia at the blockades on the Macedonian-Greek border on 21 April 1990 (Petrov 2017). The blockades were organized by the World Macedonian Congress, agitating for the abolition of visas, affirmation of the position and rights of the Macedonians in Greece, and citizenship, civil, and hereditary rights for Macedonians forcibly expelled from the Aegean part of Macedonia from the Balkan Wars to the Greek Civil War.[41] Ljupčo Arsov, assistant foreign minister and former consul in the Consulate General of Yugoslavia in Thessaloniki, recalled that the Kutleš sun appeared on a map of ethnic Macedonia which arrived from Australia at the airport in Skopje during the breakup of Yugoslavia in 1990–91.

The popularity of the lion grew quickly. On 1 August 1990 in *Nova Makedonija* Matkovski expressed his opinion that the land coat of arms of Macedonia should be the coat of arms of the Republic of Macedonia. Some supported this but others opposed it, believing that the current coat of arms of the Socialist Republic of Macedonia perfectly represented the characteristics of Macedonia and that acceptance of the lion would mean rejection of the red

---

[39] https://www.aigai.gr/en/explore/museum/royal/grave/of/philip/aiges/vergina. Accessed on 26.6.2017.

[40] Later, Greece would use the silver (and later golden) sun on a blue flag for "its" Macedonia, creating a completely different flag which is heraldically correct and vexillographically successful.

[41] https://m.facebook.com/SvetskiMakedonskiKongres/posts/1197936780219928?locale2=id_ID. Accessed on 8.3.2018.

five-pointed star, and therefore rejection of the NLW (1941–1945) and the people's revolution, as well as accepting the assertion of their eastern neighbors that all residents of the Socialist Republic of Macedonia were Bulgarians (Беличанец 1990). Matkovski asserted that "the lion has already been accepted by the masses and should only be made official" (Матковски 1990b).

Excerpts from *The Coats of Arms of Macedonia* were published in daily newspapers and weekly magazines, which raised the awareness of the historical Macedonian coat of arms (Д. Б. 1992), thus promoting the lion as a Macedonian symbol. In open letters to newspapers, an increasing number of citizens gave suggestions for a state coat of arms with a lion. Many readers sent letters defending the proposal to place the lion on the state coat of arms (Лавот на грб, n.d.).

The lion became more and more important in the public sphere. In such circumstances, many companies endeavored to include the symbol in their marketing—to use the lion as a logo. Skopje Brewery engaged architect Miroslav Grčev to design a new logo based on a lion (Грчев 2005.17) (Fig. 26). In the end, however, that design was not adopted. Grčev reworked the design as the emblem of the airline Palair Macedonia (Fig. 27), which flew the gold lion in the sky as early as 1991—one of its Fokker aircraft was painted red with the gold lion.

Figure 26 – Proposal for the logo of Skopje Brewery, M. Grčev   **Figure 27 – Logo of Palair Macedonia, M. Grčev**

During the summer of 1991, as the Yugoslav People's Army disintegrated, soldiers would often place their own national insignia on their helmets over the five-pointed Yugoslav star. Serbian soldiers used the pre-1941 Yugoslavian Royal Army cockade; Croatian soldiers used the checkered field, using easily acquired stickers. A Macedonian soldier on leave, Goranče Panov, returning on a Palair Macedonia flight to his military position on Kozjak (the mountain above Split, Croatia), cut the lion from his Palair Macedonia airline ticket and stuck it on his helmet (Јоновски 2015, 161). This marked the beginning of the perception of the lion as a national symbol among individuals.

A small number of flags with the Kutleš sun and a lion flew at the 8 September 1991 rally in Skopje during the proclamation of the results of the Independence Referendum (Референдум во Македонија 1991). This demonstrates the process through which these slowly entered the public space and began to be perceived as national symbols in the Republic of Macedonia. Their popularity would increase significantly the following year when the election on state symbols took place, followed closely by the public.

3.1. The Sun and the Lion Symbolizing Political Parties

Initially, without parliamentary capacity and tradition, the ideological attributes of the new parties (such as social-democratic, liberal, etc.) were foreign to citizens, and thus parties were recognized primarily by their cultural and symbolic aspects—which celebrations were observed, which heroes were glorified, to what historical traditions they belonged (Христова 2011, 90). Therefore, parties needed symbols to help communicate those aspects. The parties on the right (often nationalist and ethnically focused) generally used national symbols—the gold lion of the land arms of Macedonia and the gold 16-rayed sun on a red field—in their emblems. The parties in the center and on the left mainly used ideological emblems, including general symbols such as stars or the color blue, associated with some ideological concept (Popovski 2005, 15).

The first political organization in Macedonia ("Movement for All-Macedonian Action" — MAAK) was formed in Skopje on 4 February 1990, with a national/ethnic symbol to attract cultural activists, and Ante Popovski as its president. The party symbol was *a gold lion on red* with "MAAK" above it on the shield (Fig. 28). The design of the lion came from the 1620 Belgrade Armorial. The flag is a black-red-black tricolor with a gold bar in the lower stripe and a linear-type sun in the center.

Figure 28 – Coat of arms and flag of MAAK   **Figure 29 – Sticker with the arms and the table flag of VMRO-DPMNE**

The iconography of the founding congress of VMRO-DPMNE on 17 June in Skopje and at other congresses was replete with representations of the land arms from Matkovski's book and different flags with a lion and the sun. In the autumn of 1991, VMRO-DPMNE chose a specific symbol—a coat of arms with *a gold crowned lion with a split tail on red*, a design based on the land arms of Macedonia from the Belgrade Armorial of 1620 and from the Althan Armorial of 1614 (Лавовска 2000) (Fig. 29). Above the shield is a red ribbon, and a disk bearing a 16-rayed sun overlapping and above the ribbon between the dates *1893* and *1990*. Below the shield, a ribbon reads "VMRO DPMNE." Zvonimir Stankovski, the secretary of the party, designed the arms, reporting that the lion was popular in Canada and the sun in Australia. So in Europe the two symbols were combined (Stankovski 2016).

In February 1991, the VMRO-Democratic Party, headed by Vladimir Golubovski, broke away from VMRO-DPMNE. The symbol of the party retained Stankovski's lion as two supporters (Fig. 30). On the shield, the map of ethnic Macedonia bears a letter M; above it is a 16-rayed sun.

Stankovski's lion would become known as the "VMRO lion" and be used by other parties, primarily those splitting from VMRO-DPMNE. Thus, VMRO Vistinska (the True One), formed by Boris Zmejkovski in 2000, simply assumed VMRO's "old" coat of arms (before the 1998 change) with a 16-rayed sun above the shield, just altering the text on the ribbons: the upper to "VMRO" and the bottom from "VMRO-DPMNE" to "Makedonija." This would lead to a court case between the two parties about the symbols.

Figure 30– Logo of VMRO-DP   **Figure 31 – VMRO-NP flag with the coat of arms**

The same basic design was found on the arms of the VMRO Narodna Partija (People's Party), formed in 2004, but with the field quartered red and black (Fig. 31). A crown was added and "VMRO NP" inscribed on the single ribbon below the shield. The "VMRO lion" would be also found on the arms of the MAAK Conservative Party: a gold 16-rayed sun on red field with three gold lions in chief.

Figure 32 – Coat of arms of Obedineti za Makedonija

Other parties used a lion on their arms, but with a different design. VMRO Macedonian, formed in 2002 by Boris Stoimenov, took as its arms a lion based on the land arms of Macedonia from the Stemmatographias, but with a visually different form, with larger claws, and despite its mane identified as a lioness.

The *Obedineti za Makedonija* (United for Macedonia) Party, formed in 2009 by Ljube Boškovski, adopted a coat of arms with a generic heraldic black crowned lion on gold field, departing from the usual national colors of gold and red (Fig. 32).

These examples demonstrate how the gold lion and the 16-rayed sun tend to symbolize parties that perceive themselves as carriers of the prefix "national" in the context of the Macedonian people fighting for national rights, and in some places social rights.

3.2. Choosing State Symbols after Independence in 1991

In the elections held on 11 and 25 November 1990, out of 120 MPs VMRO-DPMNE won the most votes, 38, SKM-PDP (Union of Communists of Macedonia—the Party for Democratic Transformation) 31, PDP (Party for Democratic Prosperity—the party of ethnic Albanians in Macedonia) 17, SRSM (Union of Reformed Forces of Macedonia—the party of Yugoslav prime minister Ante Markovic) 11, others 23. The first parliamentary session began 8 January 1991 with a lengthy and tense discussion between SKM-PDP and VMRO-DPMNE about which anthem should open the session: *Hey Slavs*, the anthem of the Yugoslav Federation, or *Today over Macedonia,* the anthem of Socialist Republic of Macedonia (Стенографски 1991). This showed how the two parties differed in their view of national symbols, confirmed by the fact that only the Republic of Macedonia, among all other former Yugoslav republics, still uses the socialist "coat of arms"—28 years after independence (cf. Jonovski 2018).

The process of establishing state symbols began with the declaration of the sovereignty of the Republic of Macedonia of 25 January 1991. Article 3 stated: "…a new constitution will be adopted by which, among other things, the social order and the future symbols of the statehood of Macedonia will be determined" (Декларација 1991). The first proposal for determining the symbols of the Macedonian state was submitted by the parliamentary group of the SRSM—Liberal Party, on 23 May 1991. In the session held 24 June 1991, the Commission for the Political System of the Assembly proposed (without result) that a procedure for determining the symbols of the Macedonian state begin as soon as possible (Петров 1991).

Unlike the other Yugoslav republics, the Republic of Macedonia had gained independence (on 8 September 1991) under the former red flag with a five-pointed star, under which the Army of the Republic of Macedonia was formed. That was the first distinctive symbol for Macedonian soldiers. Since they wore the same uniform as the Yugoslav Army, the patch with this flag was the only distinguishing symbol (the first soldiers of the ARM took their oath under that flag on 9 May 1992).

During August and September 1991, independent MP Todor Petrov twice submitted an initiative to adopt a "Decision on Establishing a Commission for the State Symbols of the Republic of Macedonia and Appointing its President and Members." At its 24th meeting, held on 23 September 1991, the Assembly resolved: "The Assembly entrusts the working bodies: the Committee on Constitutional Affairs, the Commission for Social and Political System, and the Legislative and Legal Commission, to review this initiative and to notify the Assembly of the Republic of Macedonia of their position." However, this did not occur (Петров 1992).

The Constitution of the Republic of Macedonia, dated 17 November 1991, did not determine the state symbols, but Article 5 stated: "The coat of arms, flag, and anthem of the Republic of Macedonia are determined by law adopted by a two-thirds majority vote of the total number of Members of the parliament." The Constitutional Law on the Implementation of the Constitution of the Republic of Macedonia, dated 17 November 1991, stipulated in Article 8 that: "The Law on the Coat of Arms, the Flag, and the Anthem of the Republic of Macedonia shall be passed within the period of six months from the day of the proclamation of the Constitution." Until the adoption of the Law, the existing symbols established in the then-current constitution of the Republic of Macedonia would be used.

The starting positions of the parties and independent MPs regarding the state symbols can be followed through their representatives' individual statements in the issue of *Nova Makedonija* dated 14 December 1991 (Чангова 1991).

For independent MP Eftim Manev, the historical symbols' "past history should be covered in the state symbols. History should not be forgotten because it gives the basic mark of the Macedonian state, whose formation is not only from 1945 onwards, but dates back a long time ago." He believed, among other things, that the preservation of some symbols from the current state coat of arms would be possible only with the consent of citizens, who would declare themselves through a referendum, as well as the involvement of experts.

According to Pančo Minov, of the Reform Forces-Liberal Party: "The Law on the coat of arms, the flag, and the anthem is of great importance for the Republic, and during its adoption a consensus should be formed reflecting the opinions of all factors and subjects that can contribute to finding the right solution." He thought that consulting "experts in history and science" was necessary, saying Macedonian state symbols should contain elements that would mean affirmation, representation, and international recognition of Macedonia. Minov advocated the idea that party symbols should not be imposed as state symbols, to avoid politicization and party polarization.

According to Tomislav Stefkovski, of VMRO-DPMNE, the establishment of state symbols did not "find understanding because another concept has emerged—that the national symbols are one, and the civil constitution is another issue, and the interests of the other citizens would be violated, and not of the Macedonians." He did not take a specific position on which symbols should be included.

For PDP-NDP (the ethnic Albanian coalition) it was important that all citizens of Macedonia should see themselves in the state symbols and feel pride in them. Party representative Eshtref Aliu highlighted the need for a public competition, involving experts, adding:

> All citizens of Macedonia should find themselves in future state symbols, feel the symbols are their own, be proud of them, and behave responsibility toward them and defend them if needed. Personally, I would not mind if the anthem were purely Macedonian... Every country should have a single anthem, and today knowing the cultural, artistic, and scientific potential of Macedonia, I have no doubt and I am convinced that we will select arms to suit Macedonia and future generations, a flag that will be respected by all and the anthem which will be heard and respected by all.

For SDSM (having changed its name from SKM-PDP to SDSM—Social-Democratic Union of Macedonia), state symbols should reflect the country's multinational composition and the wishes and aspirations of all citizens and the historical continuity of Macedonia without forgetting the Yugoslav period. Tito Petkovski from SDSM believed that:

> State symbols that will reflect the multinational composition of the Republic should reflect the wishes and aspirations of all citizens. Creative work and animation of the entire professional and creative potential are needed, and a law on state symbols should be proposed through a public competition announced by the Government. * * * [T]he symbols should reflect the state-legal and constituent continuity of Macedonia and must not omit the period of living in the community of Yugoslav nations.

For SPM (Socialist Party of Macedonia), changes in society meant that new symbols should express the traditions of the Macedonian people and citizens of Macedonia, as well as their aspirations for the future. SPM's Kiro Popovski pointed out that the process for the Law on the coat of arms, the flag, and the anthem should be democratic, through a public competition with the participation of experts, saying:

> Due to the radical changes in the society, probably certain symbols that were valid so far should be supplemented or modified in order to express the historical, cultural, and folk traditions of the Macedonian people and the citizens of Macedonia, but also our contemporary development.

Only VMRO-DP believed that a concrete symbol, a lion, should be an integral part of the arms. Vladimir Golubovski stated:

State symbols should be adapted to the current understanding and should be determined through a public competition. It should be possible for the political parties, citizens, and professionals to think out loud and offer solutions that will be acceptable to all. An integral part of the arms should be the lion because it is an emblem that has a historical character.

On 26 December 1991, the Assembly of the Republic of Macedonia adopted instructions for the preparation and adoption of the Law on the coat of arms, the flag, and the anthem of the Republic of Macedonia and directed the Commission for Constitutional Affairs to carry out the preparation and adoption of the Law. The procedures envisioned conducting a competition, and from the submissions the Commission would choose proposals for the symbols and name a group of deputies from the Commission to prepare the proposals for adoption. The commission formed a working group, led by Tito Petkovski, which adopted a schedule for a public competition, targeting 20 May 1992 for enacting the law, in accordance to the Constitutional Law (Петров 1992).

The constitutional commission would extend the timetable slightly. According to Petkovski, VMRO-DPMNE exerted pressure to change the coat of arms, the flag, and the anthem. "The resistance to the arms was not as strong as to the flag—as a symbol of statehood, sovereignty, and the identity of Macedonia" because the flag is more widely used than the arms, especially by the citizens." (Чомовски, 2016).

The working group prepared an announcement of an anonymous public competition and two subgroups were formed to review the proposals, comprising members of the Association of Writers of Macedonia, the Association of Composers of Macedonia, the Association of Fine Artists [of Macedonia], and the Association of Artists of Applied Art [of Macedonia]. On 20 March, it established new schedule, adding 15 days of public discussion, still within the six-month period stipulated by the constitutional law (Петров 1992).

The jury for the coat of arms and flag of the Republic of Macedonia comprised Aneta Svetieva (ethnologist), Aleksandar Cvetkovski (artist), Kosta Balaban (art historian), and Dimitar Kondovski (artist). Aleksandar Matkovski was also proposed for the jury.

The competition, announced on 25 March 1992, requested proposals for the national arms, flag, and anthem of the Republic of Macedonia, which would "express the statehood, independence and sovereignty of the Republic, the historical traditions, cultural heritage, and the aspiration for social and spiritual progress of the Republic, the unity and coexistence and modern aspirations for a democratic society, and European and world integration." (Службен 1992).

A total of 275 proposals arrived, 239 for the coat of arms and the flag and 36 for the anthem of the Republic of Macedonia. A large number of participants offered variants for both the arms and the flag (Стенографски 1992, I/7). According to the daily *Večer*, the jury reviewed about 4,000 variants (Лавот 1992), most with the sun and a lion in differing compositions.

The Commission chose three sets of designs, by designers code-named "Feniks 92," "MAKO," and "5522" as the final proposals for the arms and the flag, and presented them to the public on 5 June 1992, (З. Д. 1992).

(a) (b)

Figure 33 – (a) Proposals by "FENIKS 92"; (b) Proposals by "MAKO"[42]

"FENIKS 92" proposed a coat of arms with a crowned lion in several color combinations: *gold lion on red, gold lion on black,* and *black lion on red* (Fig. 33a). All resembled the arms of existing states too closely, while the third violated the heraldic rule of tincture. "MAKO" proposed a coat of arms with the sun from the current state emblem, but represented it with 16 narrow divergent rays, (as popularly perceived (Jonovski 2015, 168)), and a proposal with a *red lion on gold* (Fig. 33b).

"5222" proposed a red shield with a yellow sunrise over blue waves (Fig. 34 left). Other versions placed a black sun and waves on a red shield and on a yellow shield, both violating the heraldic rule of tincture. Below the shield a red ribbon bore the text "Makedonija" (Fig. 34 right) (З. Д. 1992).

Figure 34 – Proposals by "5522"

For the flag, "FENIKS 92" proposed red/white designs in proportions of 1:2 without the arms (Fig. 35).

(1) A horizontal tribar of white-red-white,

(2) on a red field a white triangle whose base is the hoist and whose point is the center of the fly, and

(3) on a white field three overlapping red shapes fimbriated in white, the right edge of each sloping upward and to the right and ending at a point.

The largest is roughly half the flag's area, the other two appear as truncated stripes sloping upward; the right-most points all align vertically about a quarter of the distance from the fly.

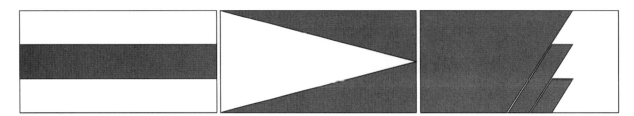

Figure 35 – Proposals by "FENIKS 92"

---

[42] All reconstructions by Jovan Jonovski.

46

For the flag, "MAKO" proposed yellow/red designs in proportions of 1:2 (Fig. 36):

(1) A yellow field with narrow red stripes at the top and bottom edges and a shield in the center bearing the Macedonian sun with 16 rays in yellow on a red background.

(2) A field divided diagonally from upper fly to lower hoist, red at the hoist and yellow at the fly, with a shield at the center bearing the Macedonian sun with 16 rays in yellow on a red background.

(3) A red field, with narrow yellow stripes at the top and bottom edges and a shield in the center bearing the Macedonian lion in red on a yellow background.

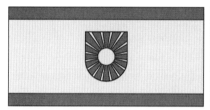 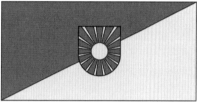 

Figure 36 – Proposals by "MAKO"

For the flag, "5522" proposed flags in proportions of 1:4 (Fig. 37):

(1) A horizontal tribar of red-white-red overlaid by red triangle whose base is the hoist and whose point is on the horizontal center 4/10 the length of the flag from the hoist.

(2) On a red field, a yellow triangle whose base is the hoist and whose point is on the horizontal center 1/4 the length of the flag from the hoist, and two horizontal yellow stripes 1/10 the height of the hoist running the remaining 3/4 of the length of the flag to the fly, set 1/10 of the height of hoist away from the top and bottom edges.

(3) Five equal horizontal stripes of red-white-red-white-red overlaid by a square of red whose side is the hoist.

(4) A horizontal tribar of red-white-red overlaid by a square of red whose side is the hoist, the square bearing an ovoid stylized proposal for arms in black, laid horizontally so that the sun (strangely) rises toward the hoist rather than upward.

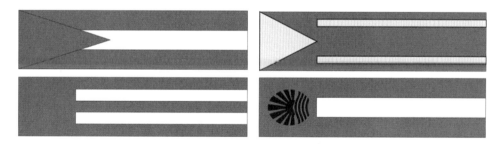

Figure 37 – Proposals by "5522"

The Commission asked the three designers to submit further proposals with the same new gold sun on a red field for the arms and for the flag. The proposal submitted by "FENIKS 92"

47

(Fig. 38) was accepted and included in the Commission's official Draft Law on the Coat of Arms submitted by the MPs Tito Petkovski, Zoran Krstevski, and Kiro Popovski on 20 June 1992, as well as a proposal for a flag with the same sun. The draft proposal states:

> The coat of arms of the Republic of Macedonia is a shield with a red field enclosed with a yellow (golden) edge. In the middle of the shield is a yellow (golden) sun. The sun has 16 primary rays that break into 32 rays, 16 of which are at the top of the primary rays, and the other 16 are in the middle between primary rays. Under the shield is a ribbon on which is written "Republika Makedonija".

Figure 38 – Revised proposals for the arms and flag by "FENIKS 92"

Petkovski, as chairman of the Working Group of the Commission on Constitutional Affairs, explained the entire process and the proposal for a coat of arms and a flag with a 32-ray sun. The only mention of the significance or symbolism was the historical continuity of the yellow and red colors associated with the flags of the uprisings. These colors appeared in the symbols of the Albanians and Turks who, for centuries, lived together with the Macedonians in these areas; also, Macedonians did not associate these symbols with an enemy, an occupier, or slavery (Стенографски 1992, I/12).

He did not mention the sun and its meanings, but asserted that the symbols were free from the claims of renewal of great kingdoms from the past. Further, he stated that the symbols did not offend other nations and citizens of other states, no foreign symbol was adopted, and the symbols would not have widespread harmful associations for certain nations and states. Finally,

Figure 39 – Generic "Macedonian lion" proposal

the Commission "considers that [the symbols] have historical understanding and are an expression of the state-legal continuity of the Republic of Macedonia" (Стенографски 1992, I/12). This is probably the only explanation of a state emblem in the world where the emphasis is on the inoffensiveness of the symbols to other states and nations, while the symbols themselves, and their intended meanings, are not mentioned at all.

Regardless of this process, the MPs made many proposals and often resubmitted the same proposals after their rejection. The first proposal for the coat of arms included a lion derived from the land arms of Macedonia from the 1620 Belgrade Armorial, with a blazon *a gold lion on red, with a split tail, crowned with a ducal crown.* Above the shield, the same crown with "Makedonija" on a scroll (Fig. 39). The inclusion of a name is not strictly permitted in an armorial achievement (Петров 1992).

This coat of arms, *a gold crowned lion on red field*, was the one most often suggested in the process of choosing the arms, accompanied with different inscriptions on the ribbon below the shield:

1. With the text "Македонија", in the proposals of Todor Petrov of 1 June 1992; Blagoj Tošev of 31 July 1992; Vladimir Golubovski of 12 August 1992; and, again, Todor Petrov of 17 August 1992.

2. With the text "Република Македонија" (Republic of Macedonia), in the proposal of Dragi Arsov of 20 June 1992; Aleksandar Florovski, et al. of 22 July 1992; and Dragi Arsov of 12 August 1992.

3. With the text "Macedoniae," in the proposal of Vladimir Golubovski of 7 August 1992.

4. Without any text, in the proposal of Todor Petrov of 8 June 1992.

The first proposal for the flag had a 16-rayed sun, now known as the Kutleš/Star of Vergina, was made by Todor Petrov of 1 June 1992. It was proposed three times, with evolving sizes of the sun (Fig. 40). The first proposal had 1:2 proportions, the sun's disk 1/5 of the flag's height, the shorter rays' length is equal to the disk's diameter, and the ratio of shorter to longer rays 1:1.5. The second proposal, of 8 June 1992, had 2:3 proportions, the longer rays 1.5 times the diameter of the sun's disk, and the ratio of shorter to longer rays 6:7. The third proposal had 1:2 proportions, the sun's disk 1/7 of the flag's height, and the ratio of shorter to longer rays 7:8.

Figure 40 – The development of the sun design through the proposals by Todor Petrov

Petrov also made another proposal for the flag: *red with gold lion*. Such a flag with a lion was later submitted by Ratka Dimitrovska on 21 July 1992 (Fig. 41a). Another proposal for the flag by Faik Abdi kept the red field but replaced the red five-pointed star with the coat of arms of the Republic of Macedonia without red five-pointed star (Fig. 41b).

Figure 41 – The flag proposals by (a) Ratka Dimitrova and (b) Faik Abdi

The European Union's Lisbon Declaration of 27 June 1992 struck a great blow against the recognition of the independence of the Republic of Macedonia, as it was conditioned on using a name that would not contain the word "Macedonia" (Историја 2008, 331). This caused great anger and protests among the population, which rose up in defense of their country's name and in anger against Greece. These feelings would be part of the driving force of a large part of the population in Macedonia, which would look to ancient components in the construction of the "new" symbolic identity. According to Stojan Andov, then the President of the Assembly of the Republic of Macedonia and President of the Committee on Constitutional Issues, the 16-rayed sun of the flag was chosen as a result of the popular reaction to the Lisbon Declaration (Andov 2017).

The political parties reached an agreement for the design of a flag with 16-rayed sun. Then, at the urging of Todor Petrov, on 30 July 1992 they agreed on a coat of arms with the same sun (Fig. 42):

> The coat of arms of the Republic of Macedonia is a quadrilateral shield with a red field enclosed with a golden-yellow edge. In the middle of the shield is a golden-yellow sun with eight primary and eight secondary rays, slightly thickened in the first half, intermittently and symmetrically arranged around the solar disk. The basic solar rays are directly detached from the solar disk, and the final outer length of all sixteen sun rays coincides with the outer periphery of the sun.

> The diameter of the solar disk is one-sixth of the length of the shield. The ratio of the diameter of the solar disk to the length of the basic solar rays is one to two, and the ratio of the length of the secondary and basic sun rays is seven to eight.

Figure 42 – Arms proposed by Todor Petrov based on the design of the flag

Under the shield is a red ribbon with a golden-yellow edge on which "Makedonija" is written with golden-yellow letters.

The national anthem, *Today over Macedonia (a New Sun of Freedom Rises)*, and the flag were voted on during the 41st session on 11 August 1992.

The flag is described as:

> The diameter of the solar disk is one-seventh of the width of the flag. The ratio of the diameter of the solar disk to the length of the primary solar rays is one to two, and the ratio of the length of the secondary and primary rays is seven to eight. The center of the sun coincides with the point at which the diagonals of the flag intersect. The ratio of the width and length of the flag is one to two (Службен 1992).

However, no agreement was reached on the arms because VMRO-DPMNE again returned to the proposal for a coat of arms with the lion as a charge. Two compromise proposals with a lion and a sun were advanced: by Todor Petrov on 17 August 1992 (Fig. 43a left) and by Tomislav Stefkovski and Gjorgi Kotevski on 18 August 1992 (Fig. 43a right), placing the sun on a disk on the crown. The change to this external ornament does not affect the underlying arms on the shield, which are a *gold crowned lion with a split tail*. This proposal was not supported by the Constitutional Commission.

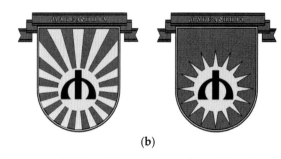

(a)   (b)

Figure 43 – (a) Compromise proposals by Todor Petrov (left) and Tomislav Stefkovski and Gjorgi Kotevski (right); (b) Proposals by Dimitar Dimitrovski

The government of Nikola Kljusev actively participated in the process and expressed its opinion on all proposals. However, a political crisis in September 1992 led to a change of government; the new government led by Branko Crvenkovski no longer considered adopting a state emblem a priority.

Nevertheless, by the end of the year several more proposals for the emblem including the sun emerged. Dimitar Dimitrovski's proposal of 25 August 1992 presented the sun with 16 narrow divergent rays similar the "MAKO" design, that could be blazoned *Gyronny of thirty-two, Or and gules, a sun-disc of the first at nombril point*. The coat of arms was displayed on a Spanish-style shield, where a yellow sun was charged with the character **ⰰ**, the "first letter of Glagolitic script, *Az*" (meaning "I"—the first person singular pronoun). Under the shield, was a ribbon with "Makedonija" in stylized Old Slavic lettering (Fig. 43b left).

Dimitar Dimitrovski's second proposal of 18 September 1992, reaffirmed on 7 October 1992, used the central sun with 16 rays from Tito Petkovski's proposal. As in the first, the letter *Az* in black was placed on the sun and the description explained the dimensions of the elements (Fig. 43b right).

Figure 44 – Proposal by Bozho Rajchevski

The last proposal, on 22 October 1992, came from a group of MPs led by Božo Rajčevski. The letter "M" was set on the sun disk; three wavy lines on the lower rays were added to the proposal Todor Petrov (Fig. 44). The Commission took a positive view of this proposal, but a dispute with Greece over the use of 16-rayed sun had already begun and its use was no longer an option.

In the process of determining the flag, the sun was presented as a symbol in two forms, both with convergent types, one with 16 rays and the other with 32 rays. The colors remained constant: *a gold sun on a red field*. There was still a difference in interpretation, the 16-rayed sun expressed continuity with the ancient Macedonian dynasty of Philip and Alexander, while the 32-ray sun was a completely new design, to be used for the future.[43]

For the coat of arms, there was a struggle between the symbols—a crowned lion versus the sun as in the flag. In the debate, nobody challenged the historicity of the lion as a symbol of

---

[43] Although present in the wider region, the 16-rayed sun, later named the Sun of Kutleš/Star of Vergina, only became popular after the 1977 discovery of the Royal Tombs in Vergina (the Slavic name is *Kutleš*).

Macedonia, but many questioned its appropriateness in modern times. Only MPs of VMRO-DPMNE and VMRO-NP (and the three independent MPs) advocated the lion. A two-thirds majority was not achievable.

The proposal for the coat of arms bearing a 16-rayed sun, matching the flag, received the greatest level of support during the process. VMRO-DPMNE initially supported it, but later withdrew its support and returned to the initial proposal for a coat of arms with a lion. By doing so, the process of selecting the coat of arms was postponed until further agreement was reached.

3.3. Proposals with the Sun after 1992

The flag with a 16-rayed sun was met with huge hostility by neighboring Greece, leading to a three-year embargo which ended with the Interim Accord to change the flag.[44]

Proposals for the new flag of the Republic of Macedonia were undertaken by Miroslav Grčev (Grčev 2011). The new flag had to be distinct but keep a thematic, visual-symbolic, and identity continuity with state and national flags, with the sun (and the five-pointed star, the sun is a star), and with the colors yellow and red. The basic vexillographic forms of the sun were considered, and for obvious reasons the Kutleš-type sun was not considered. After exploring 12 versions of the sun, the concept materialized of the sun with eight divergent rays that emerge directly from the disk, without additional elements (Grčev 2011) (Fig. 45).

Figure 45 – Some of the 12 original proposals

---

[44] The Province of Macedonia in Greece (a name used only since 1987, and previously called North Greece) began using a blue flag with a gold or silver 16-rayed sun as a symbol of "Greek Macedonia." Even though, heraldically, this is not a problem, since the flags have different colors, the Greek government viewed the Republic of Macedonia's use of this symbol as stealing one of its symbols.

According to Miroslav Grčev, the initial design had a solar disk in the middle of the flag with wide horizontal and vertical rays and narrow diagonal rays. Visually, this looked like a cross and in a few steps the thickness of the basic and the diagonal arms was equalized until a more reasonable ratio of the flag was reached (Grčev 2011b) (Fig. 46).

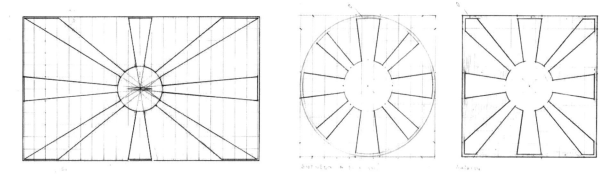

Figure 46 – Original hand-drawn images by Miroslav Grčev

On 22 September 1995, two proposals for the new flag were published, both with a yellow sun with eight rays on a red field (Fig. 47). On one the rays diverged; on the other the rays had parallel sides, similar to those on the British Union Jack. MPs from SDSM advocated for the first; the coalition partner in the Alliance for Macedonia, the Liberal Party, advocated for the second.

On 22 September consensus was reached on the proposal with the sun with divergent rays. The proposal was accepted by 86 MPs (Дарковска 1995).

Figure 47 – The final flag proposals

The proposal was in proportions of 1:2, which deviated from the original "golden" ratio and stretched the sun's rays, separating them from the solar disk by an implied circle. The composition balanced the circular symmetry of the sun and radial rays and the asymmetry of the rectangular format.

To prepare the public, the day before announcing the new design of the sun the main daily newspaper *Nova Makedonija* published a survey testing citizens' receptivity to changing the flag. The title was quite indicative: "The name cannot be changed—the flag can!" The entire survey addressed questions about the country's name and possible flag variants. 56% of the respondents did not mind changing the flag, 26% were opposed (Дарковска 1995b). This supported the theory that the flag was sacrificed to preserve the country's name (Petrov 2017).

The 27th session of the Assembly of the Republic of Macedonia, on 5 October 1995, adopted the law on the flag as well as a declaration condemning the assassination of President Kiro Gligorov two days earlier. In an exceptionally short session without a debate (showing that all parliamentary groups had already agreed on changing the flag), the Law on the Flag of the Republic of Macedonia was adopted with 110 votes in favor, one against, and four abstentions.

Article 2 of the Law states:

> The flag of the Republic of Macedonia is red with the golden yellow sun. The sun has eight sun rays that extend from the solar disk by extension to the edges of the flag. The sun's rays cross the diagonal, horizontal, and vertical. The diameter of the solar disk is one-seventh of the length of the flag. The center of the sun coincides with the point at which the diagonals of the flag meet. The ratio of the width and length of the flag is one to two. In addition, a graphic representation of the flag is provided. [Службен 1995b.]

The new flag was first hoisted on 7 October at the Parliament Building of the Assembly of the Republic of Macedonia, and on 22 October in front of the United Nations Building in New York. The flag was greeted with great resignation, as a symbol of capitulation. It was not hoisted in front of municipalities in Macedonia controlled by the opposition VMRO DPMNE until the next local elections.

The design of the flag is specific, with the red field and divergent sun. Although some of the dimensions of the sun's design are specified in the Law, some are still undefined and some deviate from the graphic representation of the flag that is part of the Law. The rays of the graphic representation of the flag are not obtained by simply cutting the diagonals of the rectangle, as written in the Law, but from a complex structure of the beginnings of the edges of the rays that form a square with a ratio of 3:4 (Fig. 48).

The flag has proportions of 1:2. The disk's diameter is 1/7 of the length of the flag, i.e., its radius is 1/7 of the height; the disk's area is 3.2% of the surface of the flag. The entire yellow sun and rays is 32% of the flag's area; the remaining 68% is red. The sun has two horizontal, two vertical, and two diagonal rays, each set with differing characteristics and different starting points, from which only the horizontal rays meet at the center of the flag. Their length is 1 unit (E) (height of the flag), their width is 0.2 E, and they subtend an angle of 11.53°.

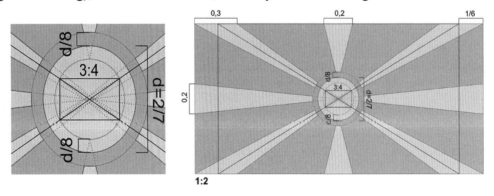

Figure 48 – Construction of the flag according the specifications in the *Official Gazette* 47/95

Vertical rays start from an implied circle with a diameter of 7/8 of the disk's diameter, i.e. 0.392 E, their width is 0.2 E, and they subtend an angle of 30.67°—making the vertical ray nearly 3 times wider than the horizontal.

Diagonal rays are the most complicated. They begin on the same implied circle as the vertical rays, but on its opposite side, that is, across the center of the circle. Their length (up to the last exit of the ray along the diagonal of the flag) is 1.22 E, their width at the base is 0.173 E, and they subtend an angle of 8.15°, which is almost 4 times narrower than the vertical ray.

The angle between the vertical and diagonal rays is 42.21°; between the diagonal and the horizontal rays the angle is 25.02°. With this construction, the width of the rays—as they emerge from the implied red circle around the central disk of the sun—is approximately equal.

From the vexillological point of view, the flag's design attributes changed but the symbols represented did not. The flag remained red with a yellow sun. The sun with convergent rays replaced one with divergent rays, it did not lose its attributes or gain others.

In the process of choosing a new form for the sun, all types were suggested except the form with convergent rays (the Kutleš-type sun to be replaced). Accepting that the sun symbol conveyed the meaning, the choice of its form was purely visual, as seen later in the study of the suns in territorial (municipal) arms.

* * *

During the secret process of designing the new national flag, matching designs for the coats of arms were prepared based on all variations of the flag (Fig. 49). All shields were red, with a gold crown above, an adaptation of the crown designed by Miroslav Šutej for the achievement of the Republic of Croatia (Stančić 2007), thus immediately associating it with the Croatian arms. However, only the flag designs were published; the draft proposals for the arms were kept secret. While the flag was finally adopted on 5 October 1995, Parliament did not pursue the matching proposal for the coat of arms (Grčev 2011, p. 3).

Figure 49 – Proposals by Miroslav Grčev

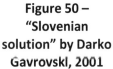

Figure 50 – "Slovenian solution" by Darko Gavrovski, 2001

The state leadership held that only minimal concessions under the Interim Agreement should be made, thinking that changing the arms might open the door to changing the national anthem, perceived as an internal affair (Andov 2017).

Proposals then followed for preserving the sun on the existing coat of arms. One was the "heraldization" of the existing state emblem, through the so-called "Slovenian solution" first proposed by Jovan Jonovski in 1998, where elements of the coat of arms—the sun, the mountain, and the river—would be placed on the shield and the wreath and ribbon removed. (1998) (Fig. 50). Several others would later make similar proposals.[45]

---

[45] Illustrations of "Slovenian solutions" for the arms of the Republic of Macedonia by Niko Tozi and Aleksov are shown, without any additional information, in a 2001 issue of *Start* (Шаровски 2001).

A second solution, initially proposed by Faik Abdi on 30 July 1992, preserved the existing state emblem, but with the five-pointed red star removed. On the flag the emblem would replace the red star. This proposal was repeated several times by Social Democrat MP Nikola Popovski in 1995 (A.X. 1995) and in 1998 (Војновска 1998) and again by then-Prime Minister Nikola Gruevski in 2000 and 2007.

Finally, on 16 November 2009, without public or parliamentary debate, the new Law on the Coat of Arms of the Republic of Macedonia was adopted, with the old-new design of the state coat of arms (Војновска 2009). In place of the red star, the wheat stalks were joined (Fig. 51).

Article 2 of the Law on the Coat of Arms of the Republic of Macedonia described it (Службен 2009):

(1) The coat of arms of the Republic of Macedonia is a field surrounded by stalks of wheat that connect at the top, intertwined with poppy fruits and tobacco leaves, which are connected at the bottom with a ribbon embroidered with folk motifs.

(2) In the middle of the field is a mountain, and in the foothills a river flows, and the sun rises behind the mountain.

Figure 51 – Coat of Arms of the Republic of Macedonia, 2009

This solution, announced as an interim solution that could lead to another coat of arms later, produced many negative reactions from the heraldically informed members of the public. They felt that removing the red star did not eliminate the ideological connotation of the arms. They also thought the adoption of the arms should occur after the scheduled referendum on a Law for the coat of arms with a lion. (This was an initiative of VMRO-NP, which organized a signature collection effort.)

3.4. Proposals with a Lion

The first attempt at an agreement on a new coat of arms with a lion was in 1994,[46] at the initiative of Todor Petrov, who as an independent MP managed to obtain the initial consent of the two major parties on a coat of arms proposal designed by Social Democrat Miroslav Grčev (Fig. 52). The *gold lion with split tail, ensigned by a gold crown* received approval to enter the Assembly law-making procedure. Unfortunately, before the session in which this proposal was to be considered, there was a misunderstanding between the parties over a completely different point of the agenda. As a result, the proposal failed to enter the Assembly session (Petrov, n.d.). In 2000 the same proposal was part of a World Macedonian Congress initiative to collect 10,000 signatures supporting a package of laws, including the Law of the Coat of Arms of the Republic of Macedonia (До средствата 2000).

Figure 52 – Proposal with lion by Miroslav Grčev

In February 2001, Jovan Pavlovski, in an interview with *Start*, described the proposal for the coat of arms with a *red lion on gold*, which appeared on the flag of the Razlovci Uprising of 1876 and in Žefarović's *Stemmatographia* (see Fig. 11). This coat of arms was placed on the

---

[46] Todor Petrov mentions 1993 in his memoirs, while Miroslav Grčev mentions 1994 in his book.

flag, resulting in the first real use of the national flag under which the Macedonians fought for freedom. On the other hand, in the narrative of the land arms of Macedonia from the Illyrian arms (*gold lion on red*), that is perceived as the "forgery" by Don Pedro Ohmučević (Шаровски 2001).

The next proposal came from the VMRO-Vistinska party in August 2001, amid armed conflict between Albanian rebels (mostly from Kosovo) and Macedonian security forces in northern part of Macedonia. The conflict was mostly around the cities of Tetovo, Skopje, and Kumanovo, and displaced many people as refugees. The proposal was based on the coat of arms of the party itself, with the same *gold crowned lion with split tail on red*, but with red ribbons above and below the shield reading "Republika" and "Makedonija" in gold letters (Fig. 53a) (Панов 2001).

In 2009, VMRO-NP attempted to collect 10,000 signatures for a referendum to adopt the coat of arms drawn from the land arms of Macedonia from the Belgrade Armorial of 1620 as the new coat of arms of the Republic of Macedonia. This campaign made no specific proposal, but did show an image from Matkovski's book (Fig. 53b).[47]

(a)   (b)

Figure 53 – (a) Proposal by VMRO-Vistinska; (b) Land arms of Macedonia from the Belgrade Armorial of 1620.

In 2014, the Government proposed a coat of arms: *Or, a lion Gules, and above*

Figure 54 – Government proposal, 2014

the shield a mural crown.[48] The red lion with no crown and a single (not forchée) tail, overcame the two problems faced by other proposals with a lion (Fig. 54). It differed in three heraldic ways from the coat of arms of VMRO-DPMNE, and the coat of arms of Bulgaria; more importantly, the Bulgarians had never considered it their own (Лажна 2014).

The 1581 work of Jerome de Bara formed the basis for the graphic illustration, with small changes to strengthen the torso and avoid an anthropomorphic appearance of the head. A mural crown with five towers on a gold diadem with rubies and pearl from Macedonia was added above the shield.[49] The blazon of this coat of

[47] http://vecer.mk/makedonija/petokrakata-i-lavot-zaedno-vo-sobranie. Accessed on 26.6.2017.

[48] In May 2014, Jonovski was invited to the government to present the possibilities for finally resolving the proposal for the coat of arms of the Republic of Macedonia. At that moment, the exact design of the arms was not determined, except that it should be found among historical coats of arms with a *red lion on gold*.

[49] In accordance with the civic heraldic system of the Macedonian Heraldry Society where, according to the hierarchy of the territorial units, three towers are for a city, four for the capital, and five for the state.

arms was changed to read *Or, a lion Gules*. The vector drawing was by Jovan Jonovski and Kosta Stamatovski from the Macedonian Heraldry Society.

The adoption of this coat of arms required a two-thirds majority, as well as the Badinter majority,[50] which was secured with the consent of the leader of ethnic Albanian party DUI, Alija Ahmeti. The lion is not unknown as a symbol in the heraldry of Albania, and is present on the coats of arms of many families and cities. In addition, the lion, as a symbol of Alexander the Great, is acceptable for the contemporary perception of the Albanians who consider that Olympias, the mother of Alexander who was from Northern Epirus, was Illyrian, and therefore, according to their beliefs, Albanian.

The final proposal was submitted to the Government of the Republic of Macedonia on 29 November 2014. On 5 December, the Government adopted the proposal for the Law on the Coat of Arms of the Republic of Macedonia. A public debate began at the Faculty of Philosophy, the Institute for National History, and the Center for Spiritual Culture of the Albanians. The participants emphasized the significance of the lion as a symbol on the arms. However, the discussions suggested that the red *lion on gold* is an element deeply embedded in the culture of the citizens of Macedonia. The proposal was to enter the parliamentary procedure where a two-thirds majority was needed for its approval.

According to a government press release:

> The proposal for the coat of arms of the Republic of Macedonia is based on the tradition of coats of arms connected with Macedonia, starting with illustrations by Willem Verland (†1481) and Jerome de Bara of 1581, which, through the *Stemmatographias* of Vitezović of 1694 and Žefarović of 1741, became the land arms of Macedonia. In the European armorials, the most consistent representation is *Or, a lion Gules*. The most famous representations are in the armorials of Jerome de Bara of 1581 and Jean Robin of 1639, which preceded the Illyrian arms and originated in European countries with heraldic traditions.
>
> The mural crown on the arms represents the republican arrangement of the state. The towers of the crown represent the graphic expression of the number five which, in turn, is a symbol of statehood. With this, it aims to emphasize and show the sovereignty and integrity of the state. Rubies and pearls are symbols that connect the country with the earth as a natural soil. The lion as a symbol can be seen as unifying by all communities and citizens, because it is a symbol of Macedonians, Albanians, Serbs, Turks, Vlachs, Roma, and other communities, and it represents the land symbol of the country, the territory, and the state of Macedonia. It has its own tradition but, also, the present and future of a European Macedonia, which takes care of its past, and also its future, through a symbol that promotes unity and creates unity for all who live in this region, a symbol that brings no division..[51]

The proposal was, for the most part, publicly supported. Illustrations of various possible applications of the arms, such as on passports, appeared on social media. One critique stemmed from a 40-year-old public misperception about the colors of the lion and the shield. Opponents of the proposal asserted that the lion was too similar to the symbol of the ruling party and,

---

[50] The requirement of a simple majority of the ethnic Albanian MPs.

[51] Government Communication 2014, http://heraldika.org.mk/en/heraldry/heraldry-arms/state-coat-of-arms/predlog-nov-grb-republika-makedonija/ accessed on 6.12. 2018

therefore, the coat of arms of the party was being made into that of the state. Heraldically, this is not true, because the proposed coat of arms differs in three fundamental ways: (1) the colors of the lion and the shield differ from that of VMRO-DPMNE; (2) the lion has one tail; and (3) the lion is not crowned. But the perception and, thus, critique, was that if it were a lion, then it must be "VMRO." However, more common were the practical comments, concerns that the updated arms would impose a cost on individuals needing to change personal documents.

Although there was initial agreement from the Albanian parties, later, some of the Albanian MPs announced they would not vote for these arms (Интервју—ДУИ 2014). As a result, the Badinter majority was lost, and the proposal did not enter the parliamentary process. Unfortunately, a political crisis began in Macedonia and the adoption of the coat of arms was no longer a priority.

The proposal was a result of research in heraldic sources over the preceding 10 years. The discovery of the presence of coats of arms connected with Macedonia—and a whole new world of coats of arms attributed to Alexander the Great in European armorials completely independent of the Illyrian Armorials—began to give another perspective. This may well slowly find its place in this debate, in addition to the established interpretation, as the existing perception begins to change (Jonovski 2009, 2013). With the increasing availability of digitized armorials from world libraries in recent years, many more people have been able to explore these armorials. Several discussions on this topic appear on the forum "Kajgana."[52]

A high proportion of the arms attributed to Alexander the Great are *a red lion on gold*, as well as the reversed of colors (Nacevski 2016). This will lead to a critical re-reading of Matkovski's *The Coats of Arms of Macedonia*. Matkovski himself included 24 arms in the book where colors are known—13 have a *red lion on gold* and 11 have a *gold lion on red*. After the publication of Žefarović's *Stemmatographia*, of a total of 10 sources mentioned by Matkovski, eight have a red lion, which confirms the actual role of the *Stemmatographia* in the heraldic awareness of a coat of arms connected to Macedonia. Thus, the strict understanding is that just the *gold lion on red* is the real and only Macedonian land arms, while *red lion on gold* is a product of a conspiracy and a series of errors, has no factual or scientific basis (Nacevski 2015).

3.5. The Sun in Modern Municipal Arms and Flags

The Socialist Republic of Macedonia had several territorial divisions after the Second World War. Then in 1965 districts were abolished and a single-level administrative system with 32 municipalities was introduced (with the capital city, Skopje, as a separate administrative unit). The territorial divisions were governed by the Constitutional Law, which made no mention of arms or flags of the municipalities, although some municipalities used quasi-coats of arms.

According to Miloš Konstantinov, in 1972 only seven municipalities responded positively when asked if they used a coat of arms: Skopje, Bitola, Kumanovo, Kruševo, Ohrid, Struga, and Radoviš. All coats of arms were designed in the socialist style (Константинов 1972). Of these, only the arms of Kumanovo had a sun without rays shown in a sunrise.

In 1996 Macedonia was divided into 123 municipalities plus the city of Skopje (Службен 1996). This time the territorial division was regulated by law, along with a first attempt to

---

[52] http://forum.kajgana.com/threads/Grabovi-na-Makedonija-Makedonska-Hereldika.26652/. Accessed on 27.7.2017.

regulate the field of municipal heraldry and vexillography. The Law allowed municipalities to adopt arms and a flag, only prescribing that they differ from those of the Republic of Macedonia, other municipalities in the country and in other countries, and international organizations (Службен 1995).

In 2004 the number of municipalities was reduced to 84, and in 2013 the number of municipalities became the current 80 plus the city of Skopje (holding a special status which includes 10 municipalities). Municipalities in Macedonia are categorized according to the status of the settlement where the seat of the municipality is located. Thus, there are urban municipalities with a seat in a city (over 3,000 inhabitants) and rural municipalities in a village. There are eight planning and statistical regions that do not have the status of administrative regions. The Law again only regulates the registration of coats of arms, without considering their heraldic qualities or the technicalities of their design and use (Службен 2004).

These two laws regulate at least some aspects of municipal heraldry and vexillography in the Republic of Macedonia. This regulation put Macedonia in the category of countries with some form of "heraldic" authority (Антонов 2008). The Ministry of Local Self-Government maintains a registry of municipal coats of arms and flags, but appears only to ensure that they follow administrative procedure.

The majority of municipal statutes stipulate that arms be chosen through a public competition. Nearly all such competitions require that "The arms should contain elements that represent the historical tradition, cultural heritage, landscape features, geographic, economic, and other characteristics of the municipality" (Одлука за начинот 2005).

Territorial heraldry in Macedonia appeared in practice during the socialist period, when "socialist heraldry"—using elements that are more ideological than geographic—had a strong influence. The most common elements were factories, factory chimneys, and cogwheels (symbols of the working class), fields or stalks of wheat (symbols of agriculture), and the sunrise (a symbol of a brighter future).

Most of the current arms depict landscapes and stray far from classical heraldry. In a 2015 study, municipal coats of arms in Macedonia were classified into four categories according to their heraldic potential:

1. Heraldic—coats of arms, according to the Macedonian Civic Heraldic System of the Macedonian Heraldry Society, considered heraldic or could become so with only minor changes (15 arms or 18%);

2. Potentially heraldic—coats of arms with heraldic elements that need to be provided with a heraldic blazon (nine arms or 11%);

3. Arms with some heraldic potential arms that could be emblazoned heraldically following the removal of non-heraldic items such as text and text scrolls bearing the name of the municipality (six arms or 7%); and

4. Those impossible to consider heraldic (52 arms or 65%) (cf. Јоновски, 2015, 189–222).

While the flags of local self-government units in the Republic of Macedonia are diverse in their type and inspiration, most have monochrome or multi-colored fields bearing the municipal coat of arms. Most were chosen through public competitions, which often required that the flag use the arms (Одлука 2005), and most have proportions of 1:2, also often a requirement.

The full coat of arms appears on 53 flags (68%), of which 26 have a monochrome field in the colors of white (10), red (8), blue (6), and yellow (2) (the flag of the city of Skopje falls into this category); 20 flags have bicolor fields in red-yellow (7), blue-white (6), red-blue (2), red-black (2), red-white (2), and green-yellow (1); and 7 flags have three or more colors (Јоновски 2015, 270).

Some elements of the arms appear on another 13 flags, while 12 flags do not use the arms or any elements at all. Flags with three colors use yellow, black, and red (4), yellow, red, and green (2), and other combinations (one each).

The sun, a symbol of the "brighter future" in the socialist period, dominates the coats of arms of the municipalities, and therefore the flags. Other flags contain sun rays. Landscapes appear on 31; 19 are quasi-heraldic and 11 appear in logos. But the most frequent charge is the sun, appearing on 33 of the arms and 35 of the flags, for a combined total of 37 arms or flags with the sun.

The sun in municipal heraldry and vexillography

In heraldry the sun is normally represented in only one way, the "sun in splendor". It is commonly represented by a disk from which alternating straight and wavy rays emanate (the disk may have the features of a human face). The number of rays, which always emerge directly from the disk, can vary (Brooke-Little 1996, 198).

Various types of suns similar to those that appear on flags appear in current Macedonian municipal arms and therefore should be considered vexillological representations of the sun.

The Dictionary of Vexillology on the FOTW (Flags of the World) website illustrates five types of sun:

1. The Sun in Splendor—the heraldic sun;

2. Sunlight—a sun of any type with rays directly emerging from it;

3. Solar Cross—a circle with a cross;

4. Solar Disk—a sun without rays; and

5. Solar Symbol—any symbol of the sun other than the above.

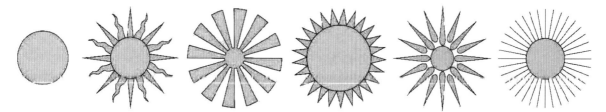

Figure 55 – Types of sun: 1. Solar disk, 2. Heraldic sun, 3. Sun with divergent rays, 4. Sun with convergent rays, 5. Kutleš-type sun, 6. Linear or socialist sun

However, Macedonian municipal heraldry and vexillography use six main types of sun (Fig. 55):

1. The solar disk—without the sun's rays;

2. A heraldic sun—the sun in splendor;

3. The sun with divergent rays—where the rays spread from the disk;

4. The sun with convergent rays—where the rays, regardless of their origins, end at a point;

5. The Kutleš-type sun, a special type of sun with convergent rays (while it can be found in many places, it is named after the sun symbol on the lid of the sarcophagus of the royal tombs in Vergina);[53]

6. The socialist or linear sun, where the rays emerge from the disk as lines.

In suns with rays, an important consideration is whether the rays connect directly to the disk or there is space between them. Sometimes rays are present without the disk, but are considered a variant of a sun disk (this is because in heraldry the sun's rays may exist alone as a separate phenomenon—when the sun's rays emerge from other heraldic figures they are blazoned *rayonnée*).

The sun can be part of a "sunrise" when only part of the sun is visible and the remainder is behind the horizon or another element such as a mountain.

Type 1. Solar disk

This type of sun appears on the coats of arms of four municipalities: Želino, where the sun, part of the landscape, is white over a blue horizon; Studeničani, where a yellow sun rises from behind a mountain on a blue background; Tearce, with a similar rising sun; and Kumanovo, where a circle (which the municipality perceives as a sun) forms part of a complex non-heraldic composition.

Among flags without the municipal arms, the flag of Vevčani bears a sun without rays in the middle of the flag, with a flower superimposed on it. The flag of Rosoman has a shield differing from the arms of the municipality, bearing a gold disk (apparently a sun) on a red background.

Type 2. Heraldic sun

As noted, the classic heraldic sun has a solar disk and (usually) alternating straight and wavy rays directly connected to the disk. The number of rays is not generally part of the blazon but subject to heraldic artistic interpretation, although the number of rays may have special importance for some armigers.

A sun of this type appears as a crest on the arms of Aerodrom—in gold with 24 wavy rays (of which 13 are visible)—but no sun of this type occurs in the shield of any municipality's arms.

Type 3. Sun with divergent rays

This type of sun has rays that spread radially from the sun disk; they may spread to the edges of the field (the shield) or be couped (and thus form an emblem).

---

[53] Suns of the Vergina (Kutleš) type have been found at other archaeological sites in the country, such as on the 12 ceramic wine glasses found near Samuil's Fortress in Ohrid. A Kutleš-type sun appears on the base of the cups. Also in the Macedonian shields in the tomb in Bonce dating from the 4th century BC (Кузман, Паско. Елизабета Димитрова, Јован Донев. ред. *Македонија, милениумски културно историски факти*, Медиа Принт Македонија, Универзитет „Евро-Балкан", Том 2, Скопје 2013, 676.

This type of sun is found in 10 arms, eight of them showing a sunrise—part of the sun is below the horizon. The suns in five arms have five or eight visible rays (Vasilevo, Karbinci, Kisela Voda, Pehčevo, Sopište). The suns in the arms of Zrnovci and Resen have 12 and 13 visible rays respectively. The sun can be found above the horizon in the arms of Butel, Demir Kapija, and Zelnikovo, where the sun is gold on a blue sky.

In such suns, the rays can emerge immediately from the disk or with a gap. On these arms, half have suns with rays joined to the disk and half have rays separated from the disk. The rays can be couped or continue out to the field. Only one coat of arms, that of Resen, has a sun with couped rays.

On flags without arms, the sun with divergent rays appears on the flags of Valandovo, Zrnovci, and Čaška. On Čaška's flag the sun has 16 implied rays, of which five are visible. The disk is in the canton. The flag of Valandovo, on the other hand, has a sun that differs from the one on the arms, it shows a circle with one beam emerging on a diagonal toward the lower fly. On the flag of Zrnovci, the sun differs from that of the arms, and 3 out of 8 implied rays are visible.

Type 4. Sun with convergent rays

The sun with convergent rays is a disk from which rays of a defined length emerge. The rays can spring directly from the disk or be separated by a gap. Rays can be simple triangles or another shape (such as a diamond). However, if the rays begin with a semi-circle, then they are considered a Kutleš-type sun.

This type of sun is found on 10 arms. On five the sun is part of a symbolic landscape showing a gold sun on a blue sky (Gevgelija, Gradsko, Debarca, Negotino, and Novaci). On another five (Bogdanci, Gjorče Petrov, Krivogaštani, Rosoman, and Strumica) the sun appears as an emblem in the field, and in two others the sun is combined with another symbol. Three suns have rays joined to the disk and four have rays separated from the disk.

Among flags not bearing arms, but showing a sun with convergent rays, are those of Novaci, Bosilovo, Ilinden, and Pehčevo. The sun on Novaci's flag consists of a disk in the canton and 16 rays of different lengths that fill the flag. The sun on the Vasilevo flag has a disk overlapping the hoist and 16 rays; five are visible. The flag of Pehčevo contains two suns, one on the flag with six rays that follow the rectangular shape of the flag, and another of type 3 in the center of the arms. The sun of the Ilinden flag is complete and has 12 rays.

Type 5. Kutleš-type sun

The Kutleš-type sun is a small sun disk whose rays begin with a semicircular base and are longer than the diameter of the disk. It usually has an equal number of primary rays and shorter secondary rays (which end at the same distance as the primary rays, such that the rays' ends form a circle). Heraldically, it is actually a star, but in Macedonia, it is considered a sun with small disk. Suns of this type can have 6, 8, 12, or 16 rays (Јоновски, 2015, 197).

The Kutleš-type sun appears on five arms (Vinica, Ilinden, Konče, Mogila, and Rosoman). All of these show a sunrise in gold, four on a blue field and the other on red. Most of the suns have 16 rays of which fewer are visible; two suns have 26 rays.

Among flags without arms but bearing a Kutleš-type sun are those of the municipalities of Novo Selo and Makedonska Kamenica. Novo Selo has a quarter-sun in the lower hoist with 12 implied rays, three of which are visible, one larger and two smaller. Makedonska Kamenica has a full sun with 16 rays.

Type 6. Linear or socialist sun
The sun in the arms and on the flag of the Republic of Macedonia is of this type.

The sun in the municipalities' description of the arms

The official descriptions of the coat of arms of municipalities, usually found in the Statute of the Municipality or other official documents, fall into five categories.

1. No official description at all—municipal officials/employees do not recall having an official description of the arms, just an image of it.

2. No mention of the sun—usually the arms are described such as: "the local landscape," "surroundings," "geographic specifics."

3. The contents of the arms is merely listed—describing the arms by listing the elements: "On the Arms of the Municipality there are: field, sky, sun …"

4. The sun is described as a sunrise—e.g., the description says: "Behind the mountain there is a sunrise."

5. A more detailed description—the content of the "arms" is described as: "A half of the sun with 13 visible rays coming out of the sun, the rays being wavy."

As for the socio-cultural context, the municipal flag and arms descriptions available present the symbolism of the sun in several ways.

The sun can mark the beginning, announcing a new existence. In municipality of Butel the description reads: "The sunrise symbolizes the appearance of the new Municipality of Butel."

The connection of several settlements in one municipality can be shown through number of rays of the sun. Thus, for the municipality of Zrnovci the three rays symbolize its three settlements: Zrnovci, Morodvis, and Vidovište. The municipality of Ilinden describes the Kutleš-type sun, which rises behind a church: "There are 12 rays representing 12 populated places, and in the middle the monastery of SS. Peter and Paul, as a symbol of connection." In the municipality of Krivogaštani, the arms "contain a sun with eleven rays with eleven stars that mark the eleven inhabited places" in the municipality.

Several municipalities describe the sun as part of the landscape. In the arms of Gradsko, the sun represents Gradsko as a warm, fertile area. In the arms of Vasilevo, the sun, on which the fields and crops depend, symbolizes its importance to agriculture, while the description "in the blue skies is given the sunrise" connects with Vasilevo's fields and the cultures there.

In some municipalities, the sun appears as a symbol of freedom and progress. In the Municipality of Vasilevo it is also perceived as a "symbol of the desire for light and freedom." For Kumanovo the sun represents "warmth, hospitality set on a red background, a symbol of revolution, youth, and driving force." In the Skopje municipality of Gjorče Petrov, the sun is "a symbol of development, perspective, happy and positive life."

Of the 80 municipalities in the Republic of Macedonia, 37 (46%) have a sun on their arms and/or flag. On 24 (30%) the sun is on the coat of arms on the flag; 3 municipalities have the sun only on the coat of arms, and 4 have a sun only on the flag, while 5 municipalities have different suns on the arms and flag. Counting these as different suns, the total number is 42.

Five types of sun appear on municipal coats of arms and flags:

1. Solar disk: 6, or 14% (on four arms and two flags, without the arms placed on the flags, which will apply to others);

2. Heraldic sun: one, or 2% (on one example of arms);

3. Sun with divergent rays: 15, or 34% (on 12 arms and three flags);

4. Sun with convergent rays: 15, or 34% (on 11 arms and four flags);

5. Kutleš-type sun: seven, or 16% (on five arms and two flags).

No municipal flags or coats of arms have a sun of the sixth type—linear or socialist sun.

Of these 42 suns, 22 (19 on arms and three on flags) or 52%, are depicted only as part of the landscape or as a sunrise. This comes as no surprise, as the sun in the national coat of arms is defined as "the sun rising behind the mountain," and the anthem also sings of "the birth of new sun"—the sunrise. Another four arms (or 9%) depict a fully-risen sun, for a total of 61% showing the sun as part of the landscape.

4.   Conclusions

Social, political, historical, and cultural circumstances have undoubtedly influenced the perception of the sun and the lion as symbols of Macedonia at different times during its existence.

The sun symbolized the Macedonian royal dynasty until the end of the ancient Macedonian state. It persisted "hidden" until the beginning of the 20th century when it reappeared as a symbol of something new, a new order with social justice but also a new national freedom. It appeared on the proposal for a flag of Macedonia in St. Petersburg in 1914, then the new sun of freedom rose on the arms of the People's Republic of Macedonia in 1946, and again on the flag of the Republic of Macedonia in 1992.

The lion appeared as a symbol associated with Macedonia in the 13th century on a coat of arms attributed to Alexander the Great of Macedon and in the 16th century it was transformed into the land arms of Macedonia. As such it was embraced by the nationalist movement of the 19th century and the beginning of the 20th century.

After the Republic of Macedonia declared its independence in 1991, all political parties supported changing the state emblem and the flag through a competition. This method helped resolve the challenge of parties disagreeing about a symbol, or that symbol being associated with one of the parties.

The basic suggestions for the coat of arms were two: 1) a lion connected with the land arms of Macedonia taken from the Illyrian arms, and 2) a new design for the sun, free from any claims for the renewal of larger kingdoms and thus not offending other nations and members of other states, not being an imported foreign symbol, and not being a symbol that would raise harmful associations for certain nations and states.

One of the reasons for not accepting the arms with the lion lay in Matkovski's widely accepted but incorrect assertion (repeated since the 1970s) that the Macedonian coat of arms is a *gold lion on red*, while the *red lion on gold* is Bulgarian and erroneous when shown as Macedonian. The situation became more complicated when the VMRO-DPMNE party took the land arms as its own, leading the *gold lion on red* to be perceived primarily as a party symbol.

The coat of arms with *red lion on gold*, from arms attributed to Alexander of Macedon in the European armorials and in the *Stemmatographia*, would have been an opportunity to align with other European countries by adopting a symbol of identification with traditional or historical heritage (Laswell's first category), and to neutralize the conflicts posed by the other proposals. On the other hand, the description, typology, and classification of the coats of arms and flags of the municipalities of Macedonia show the presence of the sun as a municipal symbol and the absence of the lion.

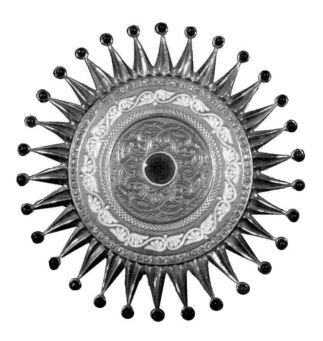

THE BREAST STAR OF THE ORDER OF THE REPUBLIC OF MACEDONIA

References

Andov, Stojan. 2017, Interview, 23.12.2017.

Brooke-Little, J. P. 1996, *An Heraldic Alphabet*, London: Robinson Books,.

Cerulo, Karen A. 1995, *Identity Designs, the Sight and Sound of a Nation*. New Brunswick: Rutgers University Press.

Ćosić, *Stjepan*. 2015, *Ideologija rodoslovlja, Korenić-Neorićev grbovnik iz 1595*. Zagreb-Dubrovnik: HAZU, Zavod za povjesne znanosti u Dubrovniku, Nacionalna i sveučilišna knjižnica u Zagrebu.

Dictionary of Vexillology: S; Flags of the World, http://www.crwflags.com/fotw/flags/vxt-dvs8.html. Accessed on 6.1.2016.

Ethnic Macedonians protest in Melbourne, Australia, 26.11.1989, https://www.youtube.com/watch?v=5Oikzkcl-g0. Accessed on 27.2.2017.

Exclusive 1988 UN-Менхетн (енгл. Manhattan), https://www.youtube.com/watch?v=sE4nhzkvzZ8. Accessed on 6.3.2018.

Filipova, Snezana. 2005, 2007, "Notes on Miak's Flag," *Macedonian Herald*. Skopje: Macedonian Heraldry Society 1, 2.

Filipović, Emir O. 2009. "Grbovnik Virgila Solisa i ilirska heraldika," *Radovi zavoda za hrvatsku povijest, Filozofskoga fakulteta sveučilišta u Zagrebu*, Knjiga 41, Zagreb: Zavod za hrvatsku povijest Filozofskoga fakulteta Sveučilišta u Zagrebu, 187–199.

First open demonstration against the Greek chauvinism held in Skopje (23.11.1988), https://www.youtube.com/watch?v=67I4ty8wtXY. Accessed on 8.3.2018.

Gayre of Gayre and Nigg, Robert. 1961, *Heraldic Cadency: The Development of Differencing of Coats of Arms for Kinsmen and Other Purposes*. London: Faber and Faber.

Glasnik heraldike, god. II, br 3–4, Zagreb, 1938.

Grčev, Miroslav. 2011, "In Search of the New Flag," *Macedonian Herald 5*. Skopje: Macedonian Heraldry Society.

Grčev, Miroslav. 2011b, Interview.

The Illyrian Armorial. 2005, Society of Antiquaries of London, MS 54, Academic Microform Limited.

Harold D. Laswell, Daniel Lerner, Ithiel de Sola Pool. 1952, *The Comparative Study of Symbols. An Introduction*, *Hoover Institute Studies*. Stanford University Press.

Hatzopoulos, M. B. & L. D. Lukopoluos. 1980, *Philip of Macedon*, Athens.

Heimer, *Željko. Exploring Vexillology through Military Units Flags*, Zagreb, Croatian Heraldic & Vexillological Asssociation, 2016.

Jonovski, Jovan. 2009a, "The Coat of Arms of Macedonia," *Macedonian Herald* 3.

Jonovski, Jovan. 2009b, "Heraldic Analysis of the Shields from Nerezi," *Macedonian Herald* 3.

Jonovski, Jovan. 2018, "The Coats of Arms and Other Forms of State Emblem Proposed for the Republic of Macedonia, and the Process of Their Adoption, 1992–2014." *Genealogy* 2018, 2, 52.

Laqueur, Walter. 2009, "IMRO", *Warfare: A historical and critical study*. New Brunswick (NJ): Transaction Publishers.

Macedonian protest in Australia and America, 1988, https://www.youtube.com/watch?v=nqfmJjjixwM. Accessed on 27.2.2017.

Macedonian Protest for Human Rights in Greece, Toronto, 1990 #1, https://www.youtube.com/watch?v=Feq-rsifj60. Accessed on 27.2.2017.

Macedonian Protest in Skopje, Macedonia 1990b, https://www.youtube.com/watch?v=IIvmxc_rnL3w. Accessed on 27.2.2017.

Medieval Alexander Bibliographies compiled and annotated by Emily Rebekah Huber, http://www.library.rochester.edu/robbins/medieval-alexander. Accessed on 17.1.2017.

Miletić Franjo (obr). 2005, *Fojnički grbovnik, sa propratnim tekstom*. Sarajevo: Rabić.

Nacevski, Ivan. 2015, "The relation between the red and the gold lion in the work 'Coats of Arms of Macedonia' by Academician Aleksandar Matkovski," *Macedonian Herald* 9.

Nacevski, Ivan. 2016, "Blazon of the lion in the attributed arms of Alexander III of Macedonia", *Macedonian Herald* 10.

Norris, J. Lacy, Geoffrey Ashe, Debra N. Mancoff. 1997, *The Arthurian Handbook*. New York: Garland Publishing.

Nowell, Kristin, Peter Jackson. 1996,, "Panthera Leo," *Wild Cats: Status Survey and Conservation Action Plan*. Gland: IUCN/SSC Cat Specialist Group, , Switzerland, .

Packer, Craig, Jean Clottes. 2000, *"When Lions Ruled France," Natural History, November 2000,*.

Panthera leo, http://www.iucnredlist.org/details/15951/0. Accessed on 3.6.2016.

Pavlovska, Eftimia. 2012, *The Coins and the Monetary Systems in Macedonia*. Skopje: National Bank of the Republic of Macedonia.

Petrov, Todor. n.d., Interview.

Petrov, Todor. 2017, Interview, 2.12.2017.

Popovski, Valentin. 2005, "Emblems of the Political Parties in the Republic of Macedonia," *Macedonain Herald* 1.

Pribichevich, Stoyan. 1982, *Macedonia, Its People and History*. University Park (PA): Pennsylvania State University Press.

Stančić, Nikša. 2007, "How the Coat of Arms of the Republic of Croatia Was Created," *Grb and Zastava* 1, Zagreb: HGDZ.

Stankovski, Zvonimir. 2016, Interview, 23.8.2016.

Stoneman, Richard. 2008, *Alexander the Great, A Life in Legend*. New Haven (CT): Yale University Press.

Tuđman, Ankica (ur.). 1994, *Hrvatsko ratno znakovlje—Domovinski rat 1991–1992 (1)*, Zagreb: Piramida 256—AKD Hrvatski tiskarski zavod.

Анѓелкоска, Лена. 2005, „Христофер Жефаровиќ", *Македонски хералд 1*.

Антољак, Стјепан. 1966, *Помошни историски науки*. Скопје: Универзитет во Скопје.

Антонов Стоjан. 2008, БХВО, 15.10.2008.

Апостолов, Мајк. 1976, Писмо до „Македонска нација" од 1.1.1976.

Апостолова Е., 2009, „Компаративната анализа на керамопластичната декорација на фасадите на средновеконите цркви во периодот XII–XIV век со мотиви од народните везови во Македонија", *Македонски фолклор*, XXXV/67, Скопје.

Арсовски, Миодраг- Болто. 1986, „Изворни документи за дејноста на организацијата ВМРО во Куманово и на Кумановската реонска чета", *Беседа*, г. XIII. бр. 36, Куманово, 1986, 76–79.

Ацовић, Драгомир. 2008, *Хералдика и Срби*. Београд: Завод за уџбенике.

А.Х. 1995 „За грбот „Ослободен од идеолошки симболи...", *Дело*, 24.4.1995.

Беличанец, Илија, 1990, „Заслужува ли лавот да се најде на македонскиот грб", *Нова Македонија*, 29.8.1990.

Билтен 1941a. *Билтен главног штаба народно-ослободилачких партизанских одреда Југославије*, 10 VIII 1941, број 1, 1.

Билтен. 1941b, *Билтен главног штаба народно-ослободилачких партизанских одреда Југославије*, 1 XI 1941, број 7 и 8.

Богдановски, Драган. 1989, Писмо од НОФМ Женева, 21.12.1989.

Војновска, Оливера. 2009, „Падна петокраката од државниот грб", *Утрински весник*, 17.11.2009.

Војновска, Оливера. 1998, „Ќе биде ли избран новиот грб". *Нова Македонија*, 4.4.1998.

Вражиновски, Танас. 2015, *Македонската народна религија*. Скопје: Силсон.

Вчера 1946, „Вчера започна второто редовно заседание на уставотворното собрание на Народна Република Македонија", *Нова Македонија*, 25.12.1946.

Грбовите на Македонија, (2) телевизија А1, 1:47, https://www.youtube.com/watch?v=hF5CGxmTi2A&t=200s. Accessed on 1.6.2017.

Грчев, Мирослав. 2005, *Знаци и орнаменти*. Скопје: Музеј на современа уметност.

Д. Б. 1992, „За македонскиот грб", *Нова Македонија*, 23 и 30.1.1992.

Дарковска, З. 1995, „Консензус за предлогот на новото знаме", *Нова Македонија*, 23.9.1995.

Дарковска, З. 1995b, „Името не може да се менува—знамето може!", *Нова Македонија*, 5.10.1995.

Декларација за суверенест http://www.sobranie.mk/WBStorage/Files/suverenost.pdf. Accessed on 8.9.2016.

Дисциплинарен правилник на бугарската војска, 1915, София, Чл. II.

З. Д. 1992, „Конечни предлози за државните симболи", *Нова Македонија*, 5.6.1992.

Закон за грб. 1946, Закон за грбот на Народна Република Македонија, Президиум на Народното собрание на Народна Република Македонија бр 559, Скопје, 27.7.1946.

Историја на Македонскиот народ, 2008, Скопје: Институт за национална историја.

Иванов Иван. 1998, *Български бойни знамена и флагове*. София, Издателство на министерството на одбраната „Св. Георги Победоносец".

Иваноски, Маријан. „Македонските емигрантски политички организации во Западна Европа (1956–1990)”, *Балканот: луѓе, војна и мир*, Скопје, ИНИ, 2015, 344.

„Илинденско востание”. 2017, *Енциклопедија ВМРО 1893–1934*, Скопје: Матица.

Илустрация Илинденъ, VII, 4–5 (64–65) София. 1935, 10. И 1 (16), 16, 47–48.

Илустрация Илинденъ 2(12), и 10, 2 (20), София, 1929, 1.

„Струшкото знаме”, *Илинденъ*, V, бр. 30. София, 24 юли 1925, 4.

Јоновски, Јован. 1998, „Грб – ослободен од идеолошки елементи”, *Нова Македонија*, 29.4.1998.

Јоновски, Јован. 2015, *Симболите на Македонија*. Скопје: Силсон.

Кецкаровъ, Антон. 1936, „Четничкото движене въ Охридско”, Илустрация Илинденъ, VIII. кн. 3–4, София, 17.

„Календар за 1947, година”, *Нова Македонија*, 29.12.1946.

Константинов, Милош. 1972, „Седум градски грбови”, *Македонски архивист*, број 1, Скопје: Здружение на архивистите на СРМ, 30–46.

Кузман, Паско, ред. Елизабета Димитрова, Јован Донев. 2013, *Македонија, милениумски културно-историски факти*. Том 2, Скопје: Медиа Принт Македонија, Универзитет „Евро-Балкан”.

„Лавовска битка за лавот”, *Македонско сонце* бр. 318, 2000.

„Лавот ја подвитка опашката”, *Вечер*, 6.6.1992.

„Лавот на грб!”, *Пулс*, n.d.

„Лажна политичка пропаганда на бугарскиот `Телеграф`—Ексклузивно за Република, Стојан Антонов, претседател на бугарските хералдичари”, *Република*, 8.12.2014, http://republika.mk/356404. Accessed on 5.1.2017.

Македонскій Голосъ, 1914 С. Петербургъ: Органъ сторонниковъ независимой Македониій, бр 9, 1914.

„Македонскиот грб од 1340, година”, *Журнал*, 11.10.1969.

Матковски, Александар. 1968, Отворено писмо, „Македонски грб од 1340 година не постои”, Архив на МАНУ, фонд „Александар Матковски”, АЕ 53/1–5.

Матковски, Александар. 1969, „Најстариот грб на Македонија”, *Историја*, год V.,1969, кн.1. според Архив на МАНУ, фонд „Александар Матковски”, АЕ/49/1–15.

Матковски, Александар. 1970, *Грбовите на Македонија – прилог кон македонската хералдика*. Скопје: Нова Македонија – ИНИ.

Матковски, Александар. 1985, *Македонскиот полк во Украина*, Скопје: Мисла.

Матковски, Александар. 1990b, „Хералдичката традиција треба да се чува”, *Нова Македонија*, 9.9.1990.

Миљковиќ, Ѓорѓе. *Илинденските знамиња и печати*, Скопје: Менора, 2003.

Намичев, Петар. „Колцето како составен дел од резбаните тавани од македонската традиционална куќа”, *Зборник Етнологија*, 2, Скопје.

Миноски, Михајло. „Тајната политичка организација ВМРО во Народна (Социјалистичка) Република Македонија”, *Зборник: Златна книга 100 години ВМРО*. Скопје. 1993, 244–246.

Младеновски, Симо. 2004, „Македонските национални симболи во текот на НОБ”, *Гласник* 48, 1–2, Скопје: ИНИ.

Народното 1946, „Народното собрание на Народна Република Македонија изгласа неколку закони важни за нашиот народ”, *Нова Македонија*, 28.7.1946.

Николовски – Катин, Славе. 1993, *Македонскиот иселенички печат*. Скопје: Студентски збор.

Новаковић, Стојан. 1884, „Хералдички обичаји код Срба у примени и књижевности”. *Годишњица Николе Чупића*, IV/1884.

Одлука 2005, „Одлука за начинот и постапката на утврдување на грб и знаме на Општина Карпош”, *Гласник на Општина Карпош*, број 6 од 20.6.2005.

Палавестра, Александар. 2010, *Илирски грбовници и други хералдички радови*. Београд: Завод за уџбенике.

Панов, Игор. 2001, „Расположение има, но погрешен е тајмингот”, *Дневник*, август 2001.

Петров, Тодор. Предлог за донесување на Закон за грбот, знамето и химната на Република Македонија, 1.6.1991, ДАРМ Фонд 1304, Собрание на РМ 1991–1994, Седница 41, точки 3,4,5 кутија 46.

Петров, Тодор. 1992, Предлог за донесување Закон за грб, знаме и химна на Република Македонија со Предлог-закон, 1.6.1992 (ДАРМ, Фонд 1304).

Пиличкова, Јасминка Ристовска. 2013, „Симболиката на кружните мотиви во македонската традиционална култура – генеза и развој", *Патримониум* 5. Скопје.

Поповска, Драгица. 2015, *Споменикот, меморијата и идентитетот*. Скопје, ИНИ.

Проева, Наде. 2004, *Историја на Агреадите*, Скопје: Графотиск.

„Проект на Устав на Народна Република Македонија", *Нова Македонија,* 5.11.1946.

„Произход на българските държавни символи (герб, знаме, химн)", Кн. 61, год. XIX, София, *Военно-исторически сборник*, 1946.

Протокол №8, 1941. Скопска градска општина, Скопје, 12 юли 1941. Архив на Град Скопје, фонд Скопска градска општина. [6.4.1.50/84–85].

„Револющия". 1895, Орган на Македонските революционери, София, г. 1 од 28.6.1895.

Референдум во Македонија. 1991, г. Третиот Илинден, https://www.youtube.com/watch?v=YvgyAaJjI0E Accessed on 27.2.2017.

Ристовски, Блаже. 1978, *Димитрија Чуповски (1878–1940) и македонското научно-литературно другарство во Петроград: Прилози кон проучување на македонско-руските врски и развитокот на македонската национална мисла.* т.2, Скопје: Култура.

Самарџић, Драгана. 1983, *Војне заставе Срба до 1918*. Војни музеј Београд.

Селовски, Клемен, 2016. *Од грба Александра Македонског до грба Македоније,* http://www.heraldikasrbija.rs/od-grba-aleksandra-makedonskog-do-grba-makedonije/. Accessed on 1.8.2016.

Соловјев, Александар. 1933, „Постанак илирске хералдике и породица Охмучевић", *Гласник Скопског научног друштва.* XII, 1933.

Соловјев Александар. 2000, *Историја српског грба и други хералдички радови*, Београд: Правни факултет, Досије.

Солунски, Коце. 1993, *Апостолски од раѓањето до генерал*. Скопје: Матица македонска.

Службен. 1947, „Службен весник на весник на НР Македонија", 1/47.

Службен. 1992, „Службен весник на Република Македонија" [Official Gazette of the Republic of Macedonia] 19/1992.

Службен. 1995, „Службен весник на Република Македонија" 52/95 Закон за локалната самоуправа / Law on Local Self-Government.

Службен. 1995b, „Службен весник на Република Македонија"47/95 Законот за знаме на Република Македонија.

Службен. 1996, „Службен весник на Република Македонија" 49/96 Закон за територијалната поделба на Република Македонија и определување на подрачјата на единиците на локалната самоуправа / Law on territorial division of Macedonia and identifying areas of local government.

Службен. 2004, „Службен весник на Република Македонија" 55/04 Закон за локалната самоуправа / Law on Local Self-Government.

Службен. 2009, „Службен весник на Република Македонија" 138/2009.

Стенографски. 1991, Стенографски белешки од 1-та конститутивна седница на собранието на Социјалистичка Република Македонија, одржана на 8 и 9.1.1991 година.

Стенографски. 1992, Стенографски белешки од Првото продолжение на Четириесет и првата седница на Собранието на Република Македонија, одржана на 11 август 1992 година. [Stenographic notes].

Стојчев Ванчо, „Знамето на Разловечкото востание", *Одбрана*, Скопје, мај 2007.

Тодоровски, Зоран. 2000, „Политичката опозиција во Македонија по Втората светска војна", *Историја*, 1–2, Скопје.

Томов, Јанко. 2012a, „Кратка Историја За Создавањето На ВМРО-ДПМНЕ—Активности Во Европа И Австралија", *Македонска нација,* http://mn.mk/iselenici-region/6826-Kratka-istorija-za-sozdavanjeto-na-VMRO-DPMNE—aktivnosti-vo-Evropa-i-Avstralija. Accessed on 16.2.2017.

Томов, Јанко. 2012b, „Кратка Историја За Создавањето На ВМРО-ДПМНЕ- Активности Во Европа И Австралија (2)", http://mn.mk/iselenici-region/6856-Kratka-istorija-za-sozdavanjeto-na-VMRO-DPMNE--aktivnosti-vo-Evropa-i-Avstralija-2. Accessed on 16.2.2017.

Тошевски, Методија. 2011, „Реминисценции по дваесет години", *Улогата на Владата на Никола Кљусев во обезбедувањето на независноста и самостојноста на Македонија.* Скопје: Влада на Република Македонија.

Ќорнаков, Димитар. 2005, *Македонски манастири*. Скопје: Матица.

Устав на Народна Република Македонија. 1946, Президиум на уставотворното собрание на Народна Република Македонија, Скопје, 31.12.1946.

Христова, Лидија. 2011, „Политичкиот плурализам во Република Македонија", *Политичките идентитети во Република Македонија (истражувачка студија)*. Скопје: Институт за социолошки и политичко-правни истражувања.

Чангова, Катица. 1991, „Корени и визии", *Нова Македонија*, 14.12.1991.

Чомовски, Александар. 2010, „Знамето – спорен симбол во Македонија". http://www.dw.com/mk/знамето-спорен-симбол-во-македонија/а-15045367 посетено на 23.7.2016.

Шаровски, Стеван. 2001, „Петокраката не е само симбол на комунизмот", *Старт*, 106, 2.2.2001.

Sources of the Illustrations

(Ill. JJ) denotes an illustration by Jovan Jonovski

Front cover – Land Coat of Arms of Macedonia from Korenić-Neorić Armorial of 1595; reconstruction by an unknown hand for a calendar of 1991.

Title page – Paeonian bronze coin of king Leontas (278-250 B.C), (Pavlovska, Eftimia. *The Coins and the Monetary Systems in Macedonia*. Skopje: National Bank of the Republic of Macedonia, 2012, 23)

Frontispiece – Ceremonial hoisting of the flag of the Republic of Macedonia in front of the Parliament Building. Photo by Kosta Stamatovski (zname.mk), 29 September 2017.

Figure 1 – Trihemiobol of Derrones (Pavlovska, Eftimia. 2012, *The Coins and the Monetary Systems in Macedonia*. Skopje: National Bank of the Republic of Macedonia, 17)

Figure 2 – Tetradrachm of Lycceios (Pavlovska, Eftimia. 2012, *The Coins and the Monetary Systems in Macedonia*. Skopje: National Bank of the Republic of Macedonia, 20)

Figure 3 – *Roman d'Alexandre*. Digital image from the British Library Catalogue of Illuminated Manuscripts, https://tinyurl.com/yyq7hcrv, f. 56

Figure 4 – Land arms of Macedonia from the London Armorial (*The Illyrian Armorial*. 2005, Society of Antiquaries of London, MS 54, Academic Microform Limited, 10)

Figure 5 – Fojnica Armorial (*Fojnički grbovnik, sa propratnim tekstom*. 2005, Franjo Miletić (obr), Sarajevo: Rabić, 59)

Figure 6 – Razlovci flag (http://documents-mk.blogspot.mk/2009/08/blog-post_26.html)

Figure 7 – Zagoričani flag (http://macedoniandocuments.blogspot.mk/2009/06/ilinden-uprizing-1903-revolutionary.html)

Figure 8 – Kratovo flag (Museum of Macedonia, reconstruction)

Figure 9 – Ohrid revolutionary flag (http://www.boiniznamena.com/?action=article&id=104)

Figure 10 – Kumanovo flag (Museum of Kumanovo)

Figure 11 – Flag of Macedonia proposed by the St. Petersburg colony (Ill. JJ, from Македонскій Голосъ, С. Петербургъ, Органъ сторонниковъ независимой Македоніий, бр 9, 1914.)

Figure 12 – Proposed coat of arms for Skopje, 1928 (Archive of City of Skopje, pictures, no reference number)

Figure 13 – Reconstruction of the coat of arms of Skopje, 1941 (Ill. JJ)

Figure 14 – Construction of the flag of People's Republic of Macedonia (Ill. JJ)

Figure 15 – Arms of the People's Republic of Macedonia, 1946 (*Нова Македонија*, 28.7.1946)

Figure 16 – Arms of the People's Republic of Macedonia from the exhibition of works of Vasilije Popović- Cico (Ill. JJ)

Figure 17 – Calendar for 1947 (*Нова Македонија*, 29.12.1946)

Figure 18 – Comparison of the construction of the arms in 1946 and 1947 (Ill. JJ)

Figure 19 – Construction of the number of rays according two methods (Ill. JJ)

Figure 20 – *Журнал* magazine, 1969 (*Журнал*, 11.10.1969)

Figure 21 – The lion on the flag, *Обединета Македонија* masthead, 1975 (*United Macedonia*, 1975)

Figure 22 – Logo of DOOM, 1975 (*Македонска нација*, V. 27, 1975)

Figure 23 – Mike Apostolov stamp, 1976 (Letter from Mike Apostolov to *Македонска нација*, 1.1.1976)

Figure 24 – Stamp of NOFM, 1989 (Letter from NOFM Geneva to Dragan Bogdanovski, 21.12.1989)

Figure 25 – The Soviet-style emblem of the Socialist Republic of Macedonia, officially called the "Coat of Arms", 1970 (Александар Матковски, Грбовите на Македонија [прилог кон македонската хералдика] ИНИ, Скопје, 1970, 153.)